STEPS IN RELIGIOUS EDUCATION

Book 1

MICHAEL KEENE

London Melbourne Sydney Auckland Johannesburg

Steps in Religious Education

Other books in the series

Hutchinson Education
An imprint of Century Hutchinson Ltd
62 – 65 Chandos Place, London WC2N 4NW

Century Hutchinson Australia Pty Ltd
PO Box 496, 16 – 22 Church Street, Hawthorn, Victoria 3122, Australia

Century Hutchinson New Zealand Ltd
PO Box 40-086, Glenfield, Auckland 10, New Zealand

Century Hutchinson South Africa (Pty) Ltd
PO Box 337, Bergvlei, 2012 South Africa

First published 1986

Designed and illustrated by
The Pen & Ink Book Company Ltd

Typesetting in 11 on 13pt Palatino by
The Pen & Ink Book Company Ltd

Printed and bound in Great Britain by
Anchor Brendon Ltd, Tiptree, Essex

British Library Catologuing in Publication Data
Keene, Michael
Steps in religious education.
Bk. 1
1. Great Britain – Religion 2. Great Britain – Church history – 20th Century
I. Title
291′.0941 BL980.G7

ISBN 0 09 163281 1

Acknowledgements

The author and publishers would like to thank the members of the community of the Christian, Jewish, Muslim, Hindu and Sikh religions for their advice and help.

The Publishers' thanks are due to the following for permission to reproduce copyright photographs:

Aerofilms: pages 41(C); Barnaby's Picture Library: pages 14(A) *top second left*; BBC Hulton Picture Library: pages 18(A), 25(C), 26(B), 27(C), 30(A), 61(C and D); British Library: page 24(B); Camera Press: page 71(D); J. Allan Cash Photolibrary: pages 7(B), 14(A) *top right* 21(C); Council of Christians and Jews: pages 9(E), 43(D), 52(A); Daily Telegraph: page 8(A); Mary Evans Picture Library: pages 18(B), 24(A), 30(A), 31(C), 37(C), 70(B); Fotomans Index: pages 62(A, B and C), 63(D); Sally & Richard Greenhill: pages 8(C), 38(B), 39(E and F), 41(D), 47(C), 50(A), 56(B), 57(D), 66(A and B), 67(D); Robert Harding Picture Library: pages 14(A) *bottom left* 75(C); Jewish Chronicle: pages 5(D), 16(A); Longmans: page 7, 23(C); Mansell Collection: pages 17(B), 28(A), 32(A), 25(B, C and D), 60(A and B); Muslim Information Services: page 20(B); Ann & Bury Peerless: pages 22(A), 64(A), 65(B); David Richardson: pages 4(A and B), 5(C), 6(A), 8(B), 9(D), 10(A), 13(C), 14(A), *top left and top 2nd right* 23(D), 37(D), 39(D), 40(B), 41(E), 44(A, B and C), 46(A), 47(D), 50(B and C), 54(A), 55(C), 56(A), 57(C), 58(B), 59(C and D), 65(C), 70(A and C), 72(A, B and C), 73(D), 74(A and B), 76(A and C); Ronald Sheridan's Photo-Library: pages 32(B), 33(C); Sikh Missionary Society: page 22(B); Juliette Soester: pages 12(A and B), 19(C), 38(A), 42(B), 43(C and E), 52(B and C), 53(D), 67(C), 68(A), 69(B), 76(B); Topham Picture Library: pages 48(B), 49(C), 50(D), 51(E and F), 58(A); West Africa: pages 26(A), 29(B).

Cover photographs: *left* shoes in a Muslim mosque (David Richardson); *top* Hindu dancer (David Richardson); *right* Jewish rabbi and boy reading the Torah (Barnaby's Picture Library); *bottom* Guru Nanak surrounded by other Sikh gurus (Ann & Bury Peerless); *middle* stained glass window of Jesus Christ and saints (Ann & Bury Peerless).

Contents

1.1 *Looking at religion*

Religion is a belief in something greater than ourselves. Many people find that life takes on a new meaning through believing in God.

There are many different religions in Great Britain today. You are going to read about five religions in this book. They are Christianity, Judaism, Islam, Sikhism and Hinduism.

The worshipper in picture **A** is kneeling alone at home praying. She is praying in her own way to God. Only she knows just what she is saying and feeling. At this moment her religion is a private matter between her and God.

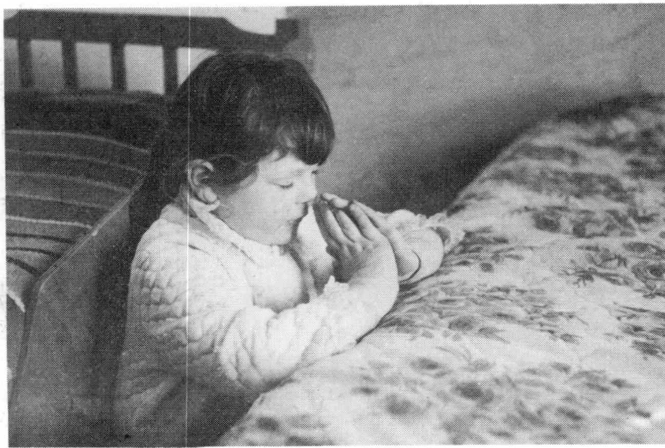

A *Christian girl praying at home*

B *Muslims praying in a mosque*

But human beings can never live entirely on their own. They belong to a much wider group of people. The girl in picture **A** is a Christian worshipping God in her own home. She shares her faith with millions of other Christians.

Each religion is a brotherhood or fellowship of believers. Every human being needs to share his faith with others and to know that others think and feel about God in the same way.

Each religion also has its own set of beliefs and ways of behaving. But most religious worshippers have certain things in common.

- They all believe in God or gods.
- Regular acts of worship are carried out to show how the people feel about God.
- Each act of worship centres around the need to talk to God through prayer.
- Worshippers believe that their faith in God must affect the way that they live day by day.
- Religious belief is a very happy activity so much time is spent in celebrating (see picture **D**).

The first four of these will be looked at in some detail. We shall look at the last one in Unit 7.

C *Sikh leading prayers*

Things to do

D *Jewish Hanukah party*

1 Write out these sentences and fill in the missing words. You must choose the right words from those listed below.

brotherhood God prayer celebrating private fellowship gods worship

- **a** Often praying is a ________ matter between the worshipper and his God.
- **b** Each religion could be described as a ________ or ________ of believers.
- **c** Regular acts of ______ are carried out by religious people.
- **d** Each act of worship centres around the need to talk to God through ________.
- **e** Religious belief is a happy activity so much time is spent in ________.

2 Here is a young Hindu describing what his religion means to him.

To me the Hindu religion is not really a religion at all. It is more a way of life. It seems to me that all religions really add up to the need to believe in God, to help other people, to be less selfish in your behaviour and to hope that there is a better life to come.

- **a** What are the four things that he believes are true of all religions?
- **b** In what way do you think this Hindu's religion might affect the way he lives?

3 On the opposite page you are given five things which most religious people have in common. Look at pictures **A**, **B**, **C** and **D** on these pages.

- **a** Describe what each picture shows.
- **b** What do all these people have in common?

4 Write down in your own words why you think most religious people feel the need to join with other people who think and feel the same way about God.

Summary

There are many different religions but all of them have things in common. Each worshipper believes in God or gods, takes part in acts of worship and prays.

1.2 Believing

We all ask many questions about life which we cannot hope to answer. This does not mean that the questions should not be asked. They are very important indeed. Questions such as these:

- Who am I?
- Why am I here?
- How did the world begin?
- Am I important in this vast universe in which I live?
- Why does life seem to treat some people more unfairly than others?
- Why do some people suffer much more than others?

For many people religion gives the answers to these questions. Of course, no one can ever prove that a particular answer is the right one. They are called *beliefs* and that is just what they are. The way in which people trust the answers without being certain is called *faith*.

Within each religion people do have their own personal beliefs. Not all Christians, for example, believe exactly the same thing. But each religion does have its own core of beliefs which every follower is expected to share.

It is these beliefs which make one religion different from another. For example both a Christian and a Muslim believe in one God, but the Christian 'Heavenly Father' and the Muslim 'Allah' are very different.

Within each religion beliefs do change slightly over a period of time but they remain largely the same. This gives a religious believer today a close link with thousands of believers who have belonged to his or her religion through the centuries. It is very comforting to people to know that so many others have shared their beliefs and that they are part of a worldwide religious community.

Not everyone believes in God. An **atheist** believes that God does not exist. An **agnostic** only believes what can be proved in this world.

A *Christian service held outside on Palm Sunday. Each person carries a palm cross and remembers Jesus riding into Jerusalem before he was crucified*

Things to do

1 Here is the basic belief of all Muslims in Arabic with an English translation underneath.

There is no god but Allah . . .
and Muhammed is his messenger.

Write both the Arabic and the English translation in your book.

A Creed is a statement of belief. The Church of England uses many Creeds. Here is an extract from one of them:

I believe in God, the Father Almighty, Creator of heaven and earth . . . I believe in Jesus Christ, His only Son, Our Lord . . . .

Now answer these questions:

1 **a** What is the Muslim name for God?
b What are the two things which all Muslims believe?
c What does the second extract tell us about Christian belief in God and Jesus?
d Can you think of two other things, not mentioned here, which Christians also believe?

2 Choose the two questions from the list on the opposite page which you think are the most important.

a Why do you think that they are so important?
b Why is it so difficult to answer them?
c Are there any other important questions which you would add to this list?

3 Here is a woman describing why she is a Roman Catholic. The Roman Catholic Church is one branch of the Christian Church. Notice that she talks about *belief* twice in her description.

There are many things in this life which I do not know much about but they are the things that I believe in most deeply. To me my faith in God is a mystery but through believing I get so much out of my faith. In the end, however, if you were to put me on the spot I would have to say that I couldn't put it into words.

Put into your own words what you think she means by 'religious faith'.

6 Carry out a survey in your class to discover:
a How many people believe in God.
b How many people do not believe in God.
c How many people are not sure.

B *A statue of the god Shiva, India*

Summary

Men and women have always found it necessary to believe in something greater than themselves. Without this belief they have often found it difficult to cope with the problems of life. Religious people often join together with others who believe the same or similar things.

1.3 *Worshipping*

A *People of different religions praying in the open air*

Wherever you find religious people you will find them worshipping. This means praising their God or gods. The act of worship may involve praying, singing, chanting, dancing or any other actions which have a religious meaning.

People worshipped God long before they put up special buildings for the purpose. The open air, with its reminder of the presence of God in nature, has always seemed a very suitable place in which to worship. For many people it still does (see picture **A**).

As each religion gained more followers, however, so the need grew to build special places of worship. As worship is an activity which usually draws many people together so many of these places were large and spacious, as you will discover if you go into a cathedral.

It is in these buildings whether they be churches, synagogues, mosques (picture **B**), temples (**C**) or gurdwaras (picture **D**) that people have gathered over the centuries to sing their hymns, say their prayers and listen to their Holy Scriptures being read. Often religious worship can be a noisy affair but it can be very quiet as with a group of Quakers (one kind of Christian) who meet together for Sunday morning worship. Most, if not all, of their worship is spent in silent thought and prayer.

The atmosphere within most places of worship adds considerably to the worship. Whilst each religion has its own rules for behaving, the basic rule is that everyone should act suitably in the presence of God. After all, each act of worship is meant to bring God and man into contact with each other.

B *Muslims at prayer in a mosque*

C *Hindu women dancing*

Things to do

D *A Sikh leads prayers in a gurdwara*

E *The Torah being carried in a synagogue*

1 Choose the correct words to fill the blanks in the sentences below from the word list given.

a An act of worship may include ________, ________, ________ and ________.

b The ________ with its reminder of the presence of God in nature, has always seemed a suitable place to worship God.

c In ________, ________, ________, ________ and ________ people have gathered for centuries in which to worship God.

d ________ worship God in a very quiet way.

e Each act of worship is intended to bring ________ and ________ into contact with each other.

God praying temples dancing
churches synagogues singing
open air chanting mosques
gurdwaras Quakers man

2 Pictures **A**, **B**, **D** and **E** show people taking part in different services. Explain in a sentence or two what these worshippers are doing in each picture.

3 Imagine you are one of the people in either **a)** picture **A** or **b)** picture **D**. Describe what you see, hear and think as you take part in the service. Here are some words to help you –

people . . . quiet . . . prayer . . . peace

Summary

If people believe strongly in God then they will want to worship him. Usually people come together in a place of worship to do this. Here they pray, sing hymns and listen to their Holy Scriptures being read and explained.

1.4 *Praying*

Praying is a widespread religious activity and is to be found, in one form or another, in every religion. Prayer is the way people are able to come into contact with God.

Prayer involves the offering of *worship* to God, allows people to make requests for help and encourages them to confess their sins before God. It can be done in public or in the quietness of a person's home. Usually the worshipper utters words as he prays but there is a form of prayer which the worshipper says silently in his heart.

Thanksgiving is a very important part of prayer. The religious worshipper feels that he has so much for which to be thankful. For example, in the Jewish religion, there is a prayer of thanksgiving for almost any event which might happen to a person, either good or bad.

At the same time as prayer is a conversation between God and the worshipper so there has to be room for the person to confess his sins. In the Roman Catholic Church this takes the form of *confession* when the person confesses his or her sins to the priest in private. It is only after a person has confessed his sins that he can ask for the forgiveness of God.

Some people think that prayer is a selfish activity with the worshipper only concerned for his own health and happiness. Although some praying can be selfish this should not be the case. Real praying always includes *intercession*. This is where a person spends time praying for the needs of others. Praying for other people brings worshippers together and unites them.

So in meeting together and praying in this way people are really expressing how they feel about God and about each other.

A *Group of Christian nuns praying together in a chapel*

Things to do

B *Extract from the prayer 'The Telephone'*

1 Here is a Muslim who is trying to describe what praying means to him.

When I pray I enter into a conversation with my Creator. I need to remind myself that I am standing in the presence of Almighty God and that one day I shall stand before him and be judged. So when I stand to pray my one thought above all others is that God is watching me and this helps me to express my needs and feelings. I ask that God will forgive me and help me to walk in the straight path that he has laid down in the Qur'an. I also hope and ask that God will continue to bless me and my family in this life and the next.

a What does this man remind himself of as he stands up to pray?
b What is this man's one thought above all others as he stands up to pray? What does this thought help him to do?
c What are the three things that this man asks God for as he prays?
d Who else does he pray for apart from himself?

2 Explain in a sentence or two the meaning of each of the following words:
a worship
b thanksgiving
c confession
d intercession

3 A telephone conversation stimulated the French Roman Catholic priest Michel Quoist to write a modern prayer called 'The Telephone'. There is an extract from the prayer in picture **B**.

a Why do you think that a telephone conversation is a good picture of praying?
b The Muslim in the previous question suggests that prayer is a conversation with his Creator. What has happened to the conversation in this prayer?
c The girl in picture **B** says she did not listen. Why do you think it is important to listen in prayer?

4 Look at picture **A**.

a Why do you think nuns wear special clothes?
b Imagine you are one of the nuns in the picture. Write down some of the things you might be praying to God for?

Summary

Prayer is a universal religious activity. It involves the offering of worship, requests and confessions to God. Prayer can be a solitary experience although it is often done alongside other people.

1.5 *Living*

To most people their religious beliefs are very important. It is not surprising to discover, therefore, that these beliefs have a great effect upon the way that they live day by day. Take the food that they eat, for example.

The Bible lays down strict dietary rules and these are followed by most Jews. The Book of **Leviticus**, for example, tells the people that they must not eat certain animals, fishes and birds. In the Hebrew language these dietary laws are called **Kashrut**. The food that a Jew can eat is **kosher** (fit), and includes any animal which has cloven hooves and chews the cud. This means that they can't eat pig but they can eat both cow and sheep. All of the blood must be drained from the animal before it is eaten. It is also forbidden to mix meat and milk dishes (**A** and **B**).

The Muslim, following the teachings of the Qur'an, is also forbidden to eat all pig meat and fat. He is not allowed to drink any alcohol or to take part in any gambling activity. Nor can he lend money on which he might hope to draw any form of interest.

Hindus believe the cow is a sacred animal so they are not allowed to eat beef. In practice most Hindus are vegetarians (they do not eat meat). The killing of any form of life is likened by Hindus to murder and strictly forbidden.

Guru Nanak taught all Sikhs that because food was unimportant it did not matter what a person ate. The everyday life of a Sikh is governed by the five Ks (see picture **C**):

- kesh (uncut hair and beard) which shows a man's devotion to God. It must be washed at least once every four days.
- kanga (comb) keeps the long hair under the turban in place. The turban is a symbol of faithfulness to God and should not be removed in public.
- kara (a steel band) worn on the right wrist to show strength.
- kachs (shorts) were worn by men originally to give them freedom of movement in battle.
- kirpan (miniature sword) is a symbol to remind the wearer of his duty to defend the weak and uphold the faith.

The Christian religion has few rules about food or clothing, but the emphasis is on the keeping of the laws of God in the Christian's daily life. Jesus taught his disciples that the laws of God could be reduced to two supreme demands:

Love God and love your neighbour as much as you love yourself.

A *Weighing kosher poultry*

B *Orthodox Jews outside kosher freezer centre*

Things to do

1 Here are some sentences which are either true or false. If true copy them into your book. If false copy in the true version.

a In both the Jewish and Hindu religions no one is allowed to eat pork.
b The follower of Islam is not allowed to eat beef.
c The cow is a sacred animal to all Sikhs.
d The Muslim is not allowed to drink alcohol or to take part in any gambling activity.
e Most Hindus are vegetarians.
f Guru Nanak taught all Sikhs that food is an unimportant part of life.
g The everyday life of the Sikh is governed by keeping the five Ks .
h The Christian lives his life by the command of Jesus to love God and his neighbour.

2 In this extract a Sikh man is describing what he had to do before he could find a job in this country back in the 1960s.

When I first came to this country with my family I spent months looking for work. Each time I turned up wearing my turban the employer turned me down flat. I was getting so desperate in the end that a relative suggested that I should cut off my hair so that I could turn up for an interview without my turban . . . I hesitated because my turban is a very important part of my religion . . . my religion means a great deal to me . . . then I gave in and had my hair cut . . . I felt like crying but I managed to find work.

a The experience of this man goes back over twenty years. Do you think that an employer today would look at a man's turban and refuse him a job?
b If so, why?

3 Here is a Jewish woman describing why she keeps the strict dietary laws of her religion.

God wants all Jews to learn to be as holy as he himself is. There are no real reasons given in the Bible for keeping these laws. I do not think that it was because the animals were unclean although it may have had something to do with hygiene. I think that it is more to do with obeying God. In following his laws I am showing God that I want to live a holy life.

What is the main reason given by this woman for trying to keep the dietary laws?

C *Sikh wearing the 5 Ks*

4 Look at the Sikh in picture **C**.
a Which of the five Ks can you see?
b Which one can't you see?
c Where is it?

5 Look up these references from the New Testament. They will help you to understand the kind of demands which Christ makes upon all Christians – Matthew 5.44, Matthew 6.1–4, Matthew 5.38–42, Matthew 6.25, Matthew 7.1.
Using the information that you are given in these verses describe in your own words how Jesus expected his followers to live.

Summary

Each religion lays down strict laws which cover the everyday lives of its followers. Many of these laws concern the diet which people are expected to follow and the food which they are not allowed to eat. The Sikh runs his life by following the five Ks whilst the Christian follows the two supreme demands to love God and to love his or her neighbour.

2.1 *Messengers of God*

How do religions begin? The answer to this question varies from religion to religion. For example, no one is quite sure just how Hinduism began. All we know is that, unlike the other religions in this book, you cannot trace the Hindu faith back to one single man.

Jewish people are in little doubt about the way in which their own particular Faith started. The Jewish nation began some 4000 years ago with **Abraham** whilst much of its religious belief can be traced back to **Moses**.

Both Christianity and Islam began when two men, **Jesus Christ** and **Muhammed**, were spoken to by God. To his followers Jesus Christ is the Son of God whilst Muhammed claimed that God spoke to him directly and that these words are written in the Muslim Holy Book, the **Qur'an**.

The Sikh faith also began with the teaching of one man, **Guru Nanak**.

Although each founder was very different there are some common threads running through the story. Jesus Christ was a Jew and in its early days the Christian religion had to work hard to separate itself from Judaism. Also, each founder was quite sure that God had spoken to him directly and that he could pass on God's Word to the people. This gave them a strong sense of authority. Each of them was a gifted teacher and, before long, had many followers also preaching their message.

One final point needs to be made. The span of time covered by these five religions is considerable. It ranges from about 3000 **BCE** in the case of Hinduism to 1500 **CE** with the birth of Sikhism (**B**).

A *World map to show approximate distribution of the five religions. In all areas only the main religion has been shown*

Things to do

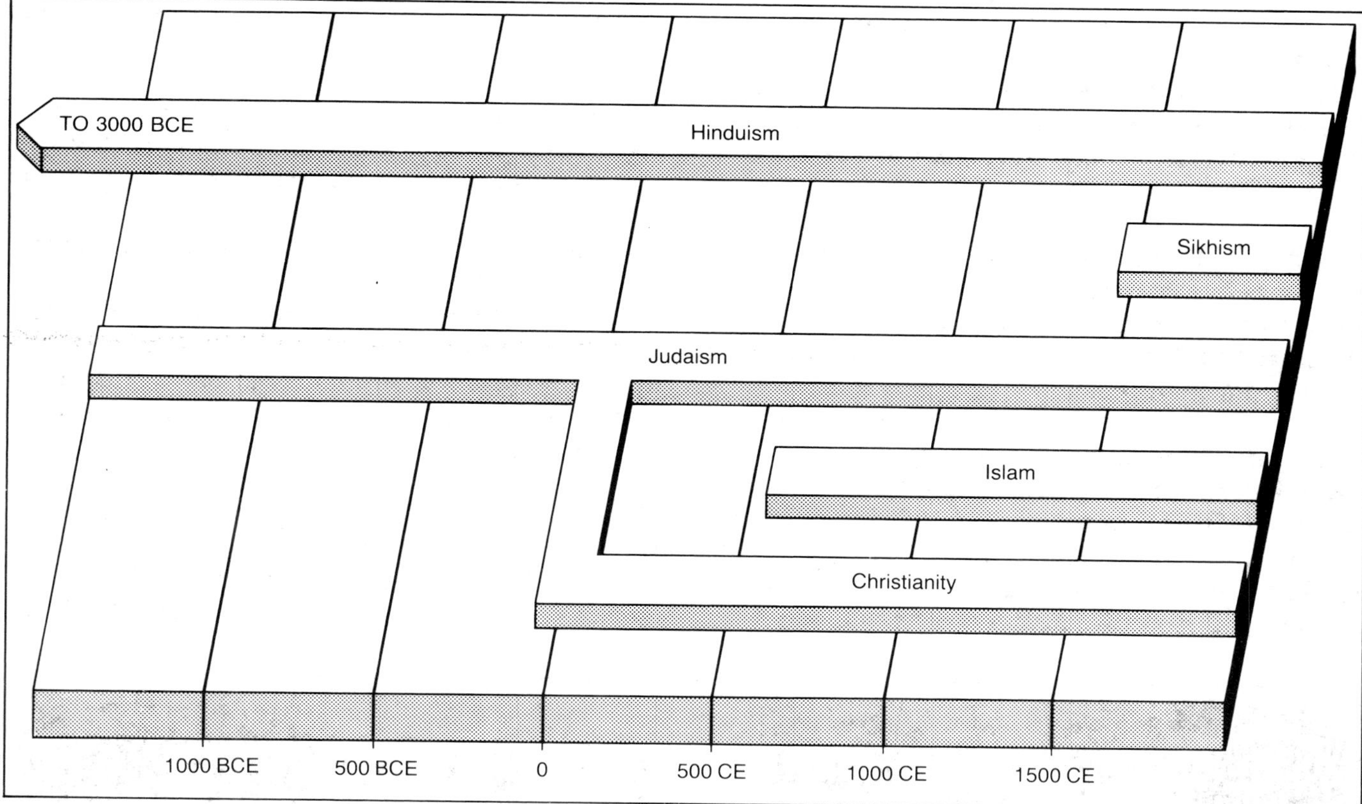

B *Time chart to show the five religions*

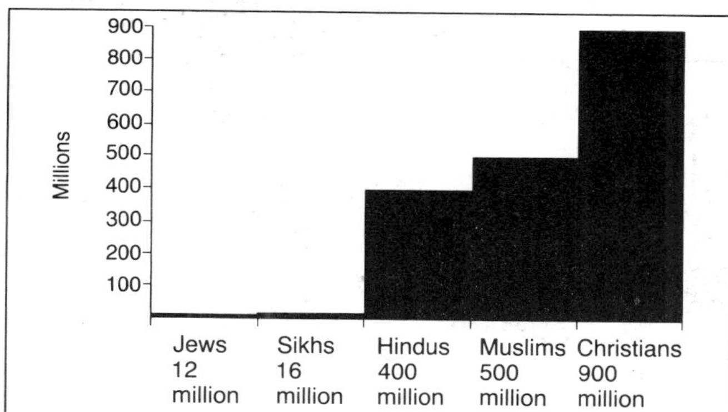

C *Graph to show numbers of religious worshippers of five religions in the world (These figures are only approximate)*

1 It is difficult to estimate how many followers each religion has throughout the world.

By looking at map **A** you can see where most of the followers of the different religions are to be found. Study the map carefully before you answer the following questions:

a Which religion has most followers throughout the world?
b Name some of the countries in which these followers are to be found.
c In which countries do most Muslims live?
d On which continent are most Hindus to be found?
e Which two countries contain most of the world's Sikhs?
f In which two countries of the world do most Jews live?

2 Using words from the word list below complete the following sentences:

a Sikhism began with the teaching of ________ .
b ________ cannot be traced back to one single man.
c ________ began with Jesus Christ.
d The Muslim Holy Book is the ________ .
e The ________ of Sikhism was in 1500 CE.

Christianity   Hinduism   birth
Qur'an   Guru Nanak

Summary

The origins of Hinduism are unknown. Christianity, Islam, Judaism and Sikhism, however, all trace their beginnings back to people in the past. Each of these individuals claimed that he heard the voice of God speaking to him.

2.2 *Abraham*

The story of the Jewish people begins with Abraham. A wealthy landowner and farmer, Abraham lived around 1800 BC in the town of Ur, on the edge of the Persian Gulf. His father Terah decided to take the whole family on a journey of some 500 miles to Haran.

It was in Haran that Terah died. We do not know how Abraham first came to believe in God. But we do know that while everyone else believed in many gods, Abraham came to believe in the one God. What is certain is that he felt that this God was calling him to make a further journey of 600 miles to the land of Canaan. It was this land (later to be known as **Israel** or **Palestine**) which God promised to Abraham and his descendants.

Until this time Abraham did not have any children and both he and his wife, Sarah, were getting very old. It took some kind of divine **miracle** for Sarah to become pregnant and for a son, Isaac, to be born.

The story of Abraham is told in the most important of all the Jewish holy books, the **Torah** (**A**). The name Torah refers to the first five books of the Jewish Scriptures. The story goes on to tell how Abraham was a very old man when he died. He was followed as head of the clan or family first by Isaac and then by.his grandson, Jacob.

To Jewish people Abraham, Isaac and Jacob together are known as the **Patriarchs** or father figures. From them and their many descendants the nation of Israel started.

But it was Moses who is believed to have received the Law from God and to have passed on to the Jews their very distinctive religious faith. A long time was to pass before he arrived. During this time Jacob and his descendants were to spend over 400 years in Egyptian slavery. The story of the rescue of the Children of Israel, as they were now called, from that slavery is told on page 18.

A *Writing the Torah*

Things to do

1 Explain each of the following:

a the Torah
b the Patriarchs
c miracle
d descendants
e Israel

2 Abraham is presented in the Torah as a man who was willing to trust and believe in God. Here are the words which persuaded him to leave Haran and set out for the land which God promised to him and his children.

Go from your country and your kindred and your father's house to the land which I will show you. And I will make you a great nation and I will bless you, and make your name great, so that you will be a blessing. And I will bless those who bless you, and him who curses you I will curse; and in you all the families of the earth will be blessed.

a What is Abraham being told to leave behind in Haran?
b Why does God test Abraham in this way?
c In what way have the promises to 'make your name great' and 'in you all the families of the earth will be blessed' come true?

3 Jewish people today feel that they have a connection with Abraham even though he lived so long ago. In this extract a Jewish man is trying to explain the importance of this link.

I have inherited my Jewish faith from the past. It might seem strange to someone who is not a Jew but I feel part of the history of my people going all the way back to Abraham.
That is why I must play my own small part in keeping the Jewish Faith alive. Mind you I don't think that there is any real danger of it ever dying out. God has looked after the Jews through 4000 years of history. I am quite sure that he will continue to do so. Today there are Jews all over the world but we are all part of the same history and the same people.

a How do you think that it is possible for someone living today to have such a strong link with events from the past.
b Who is it that has looked after the Jewish people in the past?

4 a Imagine that you had been a friend of Abraham's. Describe some of the preparations that might have been necessary in those days before such a journey could have been undertaken.
b How do you think that you might have felt after walking 500 miles only to discover that there was another 600 to do?

B *An artist's engraving of Abraham about to kill his son Isaac when an angel (messenger from God) appears. For the whole story read Genesis 22.1 – 14*

5 Look at picture **B**. Read the story of Abraham and Isaac in Genesis 22.1 – 14 and then write a paragraph in your words describing what happened.

Summary

Abraham was the founder of the Jewish nation. It was because he trusted in God completely that Israel became their own homeland.

2.3 Moses

A *Jewish slaves at work in Egypt*

A famine (a serious shortage of food) in the land of Canaan drove Jacob and his family to seek food in Egypt. To begin with the Egyptians were kind to them and their descendants but a new Egyptian Pharoah (King) decided to make them slaves (picture **A**).

Towards the end of their long period of slavery the Pharoah became alarmed that the number of the Children of Israel was growing too quickly. He tried to destroy them by ordering that all new born boys should be thrown into the River Nile.

One mother hid her son, Moses, for three months and then placed him in some bulrushes. It was here that he was found by an Egyptian princess (picture **B**) who brought him up as her own son.

Many years later, God appeared to Moses commanding him to present himself to the Pharoah and demand that the Children of Israel be released. It was only after ten different plagues that the Pharoah finally decided to release his captives.

The journey of the Children of Israel out of Egypt and back to the Promised Land of Canaan is known to Jewish people today as the **Exodus** (map **D**). It is the most important single event in their whole history. Each year they remember it in the festival of the **Passover** (picture **C**).

For the forty years which followed their release the Children of Israel wandered through the desert. During this time they received their Law from God and this included the **Ten Commandments**. These were written on tablets of stone and given by God to Moses on Mount Sinai.

B *Engraving of Moses found in the bulrushes*

Moses led the Children of Israel until they could see Canaan in the distance. Sadly he died before they reached it.

Moses is now known to Jews as the great teacher. He is remembered chiefly for passing on the law and its teachings.

Things to do

C *Jewish family remembers the Exodus at Passover today*

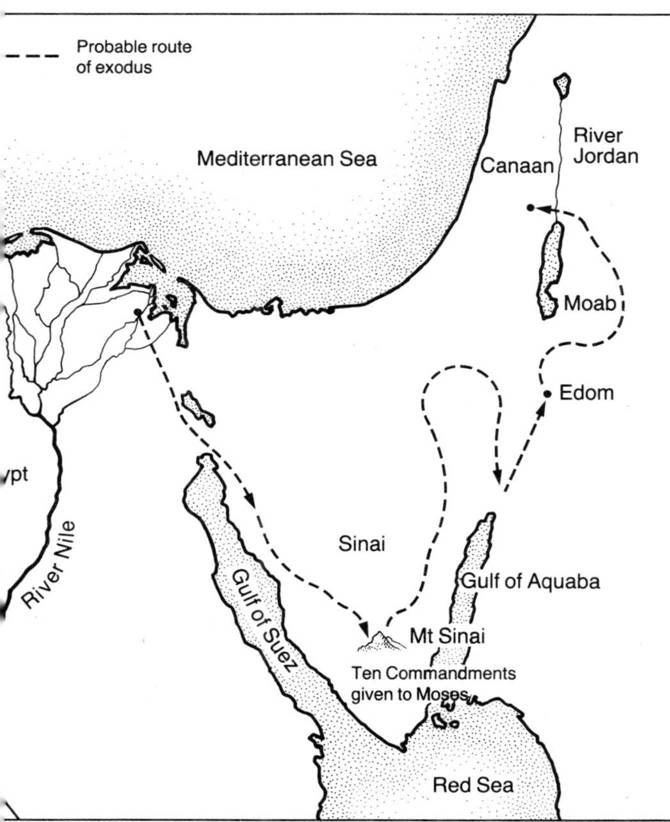

D *Map to show probable route taken by Moses and the Children of Israel*

1 Write out these events in the order in which they happened.

- **a** Moses died.
- **b** Moses was found in the bulrushes.
- **c** God gave Moses the Ten Commandments.
- **d** The Children of Israel were released after the ten plagues.
- **e** Famine in Canaan drove Jacob and his family to Egypt.

2 From map **D** do you notice anything strange about the route that the Children of Israel took when they left slavery in Egypt? Was there a much shorter route which would have taken them more quickly to the Promised Land?

- **a** For many miles the Children of Israel walked parallel to a strip of water. What was this stretch of water called?
- **b** What was the southernmost point that they reached?
- **c** From the opposite page find out what happened there.
- **d** At what point on the journey did Moses die?

3 You can read the Ten Commandments for yourself in Exodus 20.1–17.

- **a** Which commandments tell the Jew how he should act in his relationship with God?
- **b** Which commandments tell him how he should treat his fellow men and women?
- **c** Someone has said that the Ten Commandments are the best set of laws ever created for Jew and non-Jew. Do you agree?

4 Picture **C** shows a modern Jewish family remembering the Passover festival. At this festival they remember the events of the Exodus. Read Exodus 12.29–36 and explain, in your own words, how the festival received its name.

Summary

Moses is one of the most important people in Jewish history. He was the leader of the Children of Israel at the time when God led them to freedom from slavery in Egypt. He received the Law from God and passed it on to the people.

2.4 Muhammed

In the year 570 Muhammed was born in the Arabian city of **Mecca** (see map **A**). This was a very busy trading centre and was considered by its inhabitants to be a holy city.

Then, as now, a black cube-like shrine dominated the centre of Mecca. This was called the **Kaaba** and a view of it can be seen in picture **C**. The shrine is believed by Muslims to have been built by Abraham more than 4000 years ago. Today it still stands in exactly the same place and is visited by all Muslim pilgrims to the city.

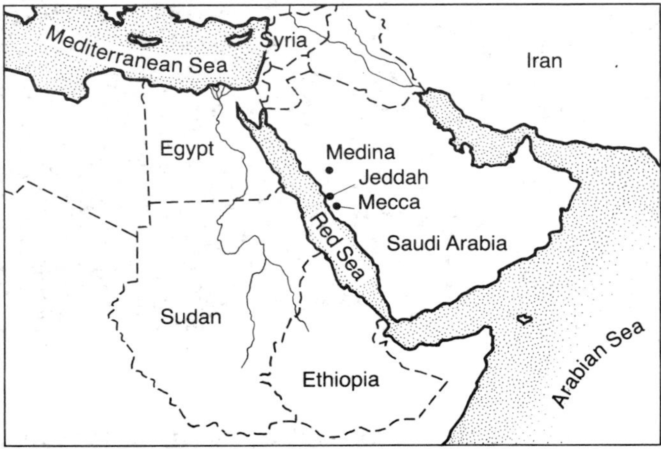

A *Map to show Mecca and Medina*

دعاء السفر

«اللّهُمَّ بِكَ أَصُولُ ، وَبِكَ أَجُولُ ، وَبِكَ أَسِيرُ .
اللّهُمَّ إِنِّي أَسْأَلُكَ فِي سَفَرِي هَذَا الْبِرَّ وَالتَّقْوَى
وَمِنَ الْعَمَلِ مَا تَرْضَى ، اللّهُمَّ هَوِّنْ عَلَيْنَا
سَفَرَنَا هَذَا وَاطْوِ عَنَّا بُعْدَهُ . اللّهُمَّ أَنْتَ
الصَّاحِبُ فِي السَّفَرِ وَالْخَلِيفَةُ فِي الْأَهْلِ .
اللّهُمَّ إِنِّي أَعُوذُ بِكَ مِنْ وَعْثَاءِ السَّفَرِ وَكَآبَةِ
الْمَنْظَرِ ، وَسُوءِ الْمُنْقَلَبِ فِي الْمَالِ وَالْأَهْلِ
وَالْوَلَدِ ، وَإِذَا رَجَعَ قَالَهُنَّ وَزَادَ فِيهِنَّ :
آيِبُونَ تَائِبُونَ عَابِدُونَ لِرَبِّنَا حَامِدُونَ» .

رواه أحمد والبزار ومسلم وغيرهم

B *Prayer for the traveller by the Holy Prophet Muhammed*

Muhammed's father died before his birth and the young boy was brought up by his grandfather and then his uncle. When he was twenty-five years old he married a rich widow named **Khadijah** and from their very happy relationship seven children were born. Muslims believe that around the age of forty Muhammed began to have many revelations (visions or divine messages) from God through the angel Gabriel.

At once Muhammed began to preach to the people of Mecca. He insisted that they should stop bowing down to the 360 idols in the city and start to worship the one true God, **Allah**.

Only a few people believed in Allah but one of the first believers was Khadijah, his wife. She died in 619. Three years later Muhammed left Mecca with his few disciples and travelled to Medina. This journey, known as the **Hegira**, marks the beginning of the Muslim calendar.

By 630, with the support of the people of Medina who had welcomed him whole-heartedly, Muhammed was able to return to Mecca and conquer the city. He destroyed all of the idols there and dedicated the Kaaba to the worship of Allah alone.

Two years later the **Prophet**, as he was then called, was dead. His friend, Abu Bakr, told the sorrowing crowd:

Muhammed was a man. Muhammed is dead. God is alive, immortal.

After his death the revelations to Mohammed were collected together by one of his disciples to form the Qur'an. In picture **B** you can see a prayer by Muhammed in the Arabic language. The whole of the Qur'an is written in this language.

Things to do

C *The Kaaba in Mecca*

1 The heads (**a** – **f**) and tails (**i** – **vi**) of these statements have been mixed up. Write them out correctly in your book.

a The Prophet Muhammed was born . . .
b In the centre of Mecca stood . . .
c Muhammed married . . .
d The Angel Gabriel . . .
e The visions of Muhammed . . .
f The Hegira . . .
i . . . appeared to Muhammed.
ii . . . in the city of Mecca.
iii. . . is the beginning of the Muslim calendar.
iv . . . a rich widow called Khadijah.
v . . . the cube-like structure of the Kaaba.
vi . . . are the basis of Islam.

2 From the opposite page write down ten pieces of information about Muhammed, the founder of Islam.

3 Copy the picture of the Kaaba from picture **C** into your book and then answer these questions underneath.

a What is the Kaaba?
b Where do Muslims believe that the Kaaba came from in the first place?
c Why is the Kaaba still important to Muslims today?

4 If the Hegira took place in 622 what year has now been reached in the Muslim calendar?

5 Copy map **A** into your book showing Arabia and the surrounding countries. Then explain in your own words what happened at Mecca and Medina.

6 What do you think that Abu Bakr was trying to tell the people when he said:

Muhammed was a man. Muhammed is dead. God is alive, immortal.

Summary

Born in 570 it was only after his marriage that Muhammed began to have revelations from God. His teachings are recorded in the Holy Qur'an. Before his death the people of Mecca and Medina accepted Muhammed as God's Prophet.

2.5 Guru Nanak

A *An artist's painting of Guru Nanak*

1 There is only one God. Worship and pray to the one God and to none other.

2 Remember God, work hard and help others.

3 God is pleased with honest work and true living.

4 There is no rich, no poor, no black and no white, before God. It is your actions that make you good or bad.

5 Men and Women are all equal before God.

6 Love everyone and pray for the good of all.

7 Be kind to people, animals and birds.

8 Fear not, Frighten not.

9 Always speak the truth.

O Nanak, this need we know alone
That God and Truth are two in one.

B *Teachings of Guru Nanak*

Nanak was born in 1469 in a small village in Pakistan. The story is told that when he was born the midwife who delivered him saw a dazzling line around his head. A local Hindu priest commented that this child was destined to become a great man, maybe even a **Guru** or wise teacher (**A**).

Nanak was married at the age of fifteen or sixteen and he then spent many years working as a cowherd. When he was about twenty-nine years old he was lost and feared drowned in the local river. Three days later he reappeared and claimed that he had spent the time in God's Heavenly Court. While he was there he said that he had been given a cup of nectar (a heavenly drink) and then told to help others rejoice and believe in God.

This was the experience which was to change the whole direction of Nanak's life. From this moment onwards Guru Nanak, as he was now known, gave up his work and became a travelling preacher (**B**).

During the next thirty years Nanak travelled the length and breadth of India and the adjoining Islamic countries on foot. A group of followers soon gathered around him and these became the first **Sikhs** (from a Punjabi word meaning to learn).

Sikhs believe that during this time Guru Nanak performed many miracles. Once he went to the Muslim holy city of Mecca. There he met a Muslim priest who objected to him sleeping with his feet towards the holy shrine of the Kaaba. The priest said that this was disrespectful to Allah (God). Several times the priest moved the Guru's feet only to find that they still pointed towards the shrine. Nanak told him that:

> *God is everywhere and is not to be found in any one place.*

Nanak chose a man called **Lehna** to succeed him. Lehna was given the name **Angad** which meant 'my limb'. A few days later, on 22 September 1539, Guru Nanak died.

Things to do

ੴ ਸਤਿਨਾਮੁ ਕਰਤਾਪੁਰਖੁ ਨਿਰਭਉ ਨਿਰਵੈਰੁ
ਅਕਾਲ ਮੂਰਤਿ ਅਜੂਨੀ ਸੈਭੰ ਗੁਰ ਪ੍ਰਸਾਦਿ ॥

C *'By the grace of the Guru, made known to men'. (Mool Mantra) The Guru Granth Sahib, the Sikh Holy Book, begins with the Mool Mantra*

1 Each of these statements is either true or false. If true then copy it into your book. If false then write down the correct version.

- a Guru Nanak was the founder of the Sikh religion.
- b There was believed to be a miracle associated with the birth of Nanak.
- c After Nanak was believed to have been drowned he was taken up into God's Heavenly Court.
- d While he was in God's Heavenly Court Nanak was given some nectar to drink.
- e Nanak wandered for forty years in India and elsewhere making disciples.
- f Nanak chose Lehna to succeed him.
- g Nanak died on 22 September 1538.

2 In a booklet written about the life of Guru Nanak for Sikh children this story about the young Nanak is told:

Guru Nanak was now about sixteen. He loved everybody and liked to help everyone. He made friends with many boys of his age. Two of his friends were Bala and Mardana. Bala was a Hindu and Mardana was a Muslim. The three friends loved one another very much. They called one another Bhai (brothers). They always sang the Guru's hymns and played together. Mardana was a good singer and the Guru loved him very much. But the Guru's father did not like the Guru's friend Mardana because he was a Muslim. He did not like to see Nanak playing with a Muslim boy. But the Guru always said:

There's no Hindu and no Muslim. We are all brothers.

- a What do you think that Guru Nanak meant when he said this?
- b Do you think he was right?

3 Although Guru Nanak did not think that Islam and Hinduism were false religions he did have some strong words to say about them. See if you can work out just what he was trying to teach his followers when he said about Islam:

'Let compassion be your mosque.
Let faith be your prayer mat
Let honest living be your Koran . . .
And in such ways strive to be a Muslim.'

4 There is a story about Nanak which tells how he started to splash water in the direction of his own farm, 300 miles away. It had been without water for twelve months. This amazed the people who reminded Nanak that the Sun was where their ancestors now lived and he should splash water towards the Sun. He told them that his farm had been without water for a long time and water was more important to the living than to their dead ancestors. Nanak told them that they should be worshipping the living rather than the dead.
What do you think he meant by this?

D *Sikh family today*

Summary

Guru Nanak was the founder of Sikhism. At the age of twenty-nine he entered the Heavenly Court of God before returning to earth. For the next thirty years he wandered around India making many disciples.

3.1 *How do we know about Jesus?*

The new teſtament.

The goſpell of S Mathew.
The goſpell of S. Marke.
The goſpell of S. Luke.
The goſpell of S. Jhon.
The Actes of the Apoſtles

The epiſtles of S. Paul.

The epiſtle unto the Romaynes.
The firſt and ſeconde epiſtle to the Corinthians
The epiſtle to the Galathians.
The epiſtle to the Ephesians.
The epiſtle to the Philippians.
The epiſtle to the Coloſſians.
The firſt and ſec͠ode epiſtle to the Teſſalonians
The firſt and ſeconde epiſtle unto Tymothy.
The epiſtle unto Titus.
The epiſtle unto Philemon.
The firſt and ſeconde epiſtle of S. Peter.
The thre epiſtles of S. Jhon.
The epiſtle unto the Hebrues.
The epiſtle of S. James.
The epiſtle of S. Jude.
The Revelacion of S. Jhon.

A *New Testament contents list, Bible 1536*

B *Illustration of St Matthew and St Mark from a seventeenth century Ethiopian manuscript of the four Gospels*

Although there are one or two short references to Jesus outside the Gospels in Roman and Jewish books they do not tell us very much about him. All that they say is that someone by the name of Jesus lived in First Century Palestine, made many followers and was put to death by the Romans. For the details of his life we must turn to the **Gospels** (**A**).

There are four Gospels in all and three of them, Matthew, Mark and Luke, belong closely together. For this reason these three are called the *synoptic* (looking together) Gospels. Nearly all of the information which is found in St Mark is also included in Matthew and Luke. It seems likely that Mark wrote first and the other two writers took much of their information from him (**B** and **C**).

Yet here the mystery deepens. Both Matthew and Luke give us details about Jesus that Mark does not mention. So it seems likely that another document existed at the time but which has now disappeared. Scholars call this document 'Q'.

They also believe that two other documents were around when Matthew and Luke wrote their Gospels. The first gave Matthew details about Jesus unknown to the other two (called 'M') and the second gave Luke details which the other two did not have (called 'L').

The obvious question to ask is how reliable these Gospel stories are about Jesus. One problem is that St Mark's Gospel was not written until about thirty years after Jesus died and the others were later still. At the same time there were many eye-witnesses still around and in those days people were used to committing things to memory.

It can also be pointed out that Mark and the other writers give us a picture of life in Palestine which fits in well with our knowledge of the time.

It would be silly to suggest that we can ever prove the details of the stories and sayings in the Gospels. The evidence, however, strongly suggests that our records of the teachings and life of Jesus of Nazareth are basically reliable and should be studied as such.

Things to do

1 A Creed is a statement of belief. Many such Creeds are used in the Church of England. From one of them a schoolgirl produced her own version. Here is the part of that version which deals with Jesus of Nazareth.

To save us men Jesus came down from heaven; he was born of the Virgin Mary by the power of the Holy Spirit and so he became man. For the sake of everyone he was crucified by Pontius Pilate; he both suffered and was buried. On the third day he rose again from the dead as the Scriptures said he would; he went up into heaven and now sits with the Father . . . .

- **a** Where do Christians believe that Jesus came from when he was born?
- **b** Who was the mother of Jesus?
- **c** Under whose power and authority was Jesus crucified?
- **d** What happened on the third day after he was crucified.
- **e** What happened at the end of his life?
- **f** Where do Christians believe that Jesus is now?

2 Read the Creed through again carefully. There are certain historical facts which Christians accept about Jesus. Then there are also certain beliefs which they hold about him. Which statements in the Creed above are *facts* and which are *beliefs*?

3 Look at pictures **A**, **B** and **C** which show pages from different forms of the Bible.

Why do you think there are still arguments today about how reliable the Bible is?

4 Here are some questions which you will need to use your imagination to be able to answer. Imagine that you are a citizen in First Century Roman Palestine and that you had heard the name 'Jesus' mentioned although you had never seen him.

- **a** Why do you think that the Roman and Jewish writers of the time showed little interest in him?
- **b** What do you think that the attitude of the authorities might have been towards him?
- **c** What do you think that your attitude and that of your friends, as non-Christians, might have been?

C *Beginning of St Luke's Gospel from Lindisfarne Gospel Book written about 690 – 700*

5 Compare the pictures of St Matthew and St Mark in picture **B** with those in the top two corners of picture **A**.

- **a** How do they look different?
- **b** Why have the two artists drawn them in different ways?

6 Look at pictures **A** and **B** again.

- **a** What does the halo or circle of light around each of the saints' heads mean?
- **b** Why do you think the artists put them into their pictures?

Summary

Nearly all of the information that we have about Jesus of Nazareth is to be found in the Gospels. From the few references that we do have outside the Gospels we know that Jesus did exist and that he was killed by the Romans.

3.2 *What do we know about Jesus?*

As we said in Unit 3.1 all of our real information about Jesus Christ comes from the Gospels. From the picture that they give Christians believe that Jesus:

I . . . was a Jew who was born in First Century Palestine. The country was under Roman occupation at the time and we cannot be certain about the precise date of his birth. The Sixth Century monk who suggested 0 CE and based the Western calendar upon that date was wrong by several years. The most likely date for the birth of Jesus is somewhere between 7 BCE and 5 BCE.

II . . . was chosen by God to announce that the Divine Kingdom had come. Directly after being baptized by John the Baptist in the River Jordan he heard God's voice saying:

You are my own dear Son. I am pleased with you.

III . . . performed many miracles. These showed the people his control over the forces of nature, over sickness and over death.

IV . . . taught his own disciples in particular and the people in general about God. To do this he used mainly **Parables** or stories.

V . . . was the **Messiah**, or leader, for which the Jewish people had long been waiting. The religious leaders, however, were looking for another kind of leader and so rejected him.

VI . . . was condemned to death by the Romans and crucified in Jerusalem. This was probably in 29 or 30 CE.

VII . . . was brought back to life in some way by God after he had been dead for three days.

VIII . . . left the earth but promised his followers that he would still be with them through his Spirit.

Throughout the world over 900 million people follow the life and teaching of Jesus. They believe that he is still alive today and is living through them.

A *West African carving of Jesus and Mary*

B *Fourteenth century painting of Jesus*

Things to do

C *Painting of Jesus carrying the cross*

1 **a** Copy out this crossword.
b Invent your own clues for each word. Write the clues underneath the crossword.
c Complete No 5. The clue is 'What did Jesus leave behind to help people when he left the earth?'
d Swap with a friend to make sure that your clues work.

2 Write down two sentences to explain each of the following sentences.

a Why we are not sure exactly when Jesus was born.
b How Jesus taught his disciples and the people generally.
c One reason why the religious leaders rejected Jesus.

3 From what you know about the life and teaching of Jesus of Nazareth why do you think he has attracted so many followers in the last 2000 years?

4 **a** We have no information at all about what Jesus looked like. That has not stopped artists from trying to draw or paint him. Look carefully at pictures **A**, **B** and **C**. Do any of them show Jesus as you imagine him to be?
b Imagine that you have been asked to paint a picture of Jesus. Think about his face, his hair, his clothes and his shoes. Describe what you would make him look like in your picture.

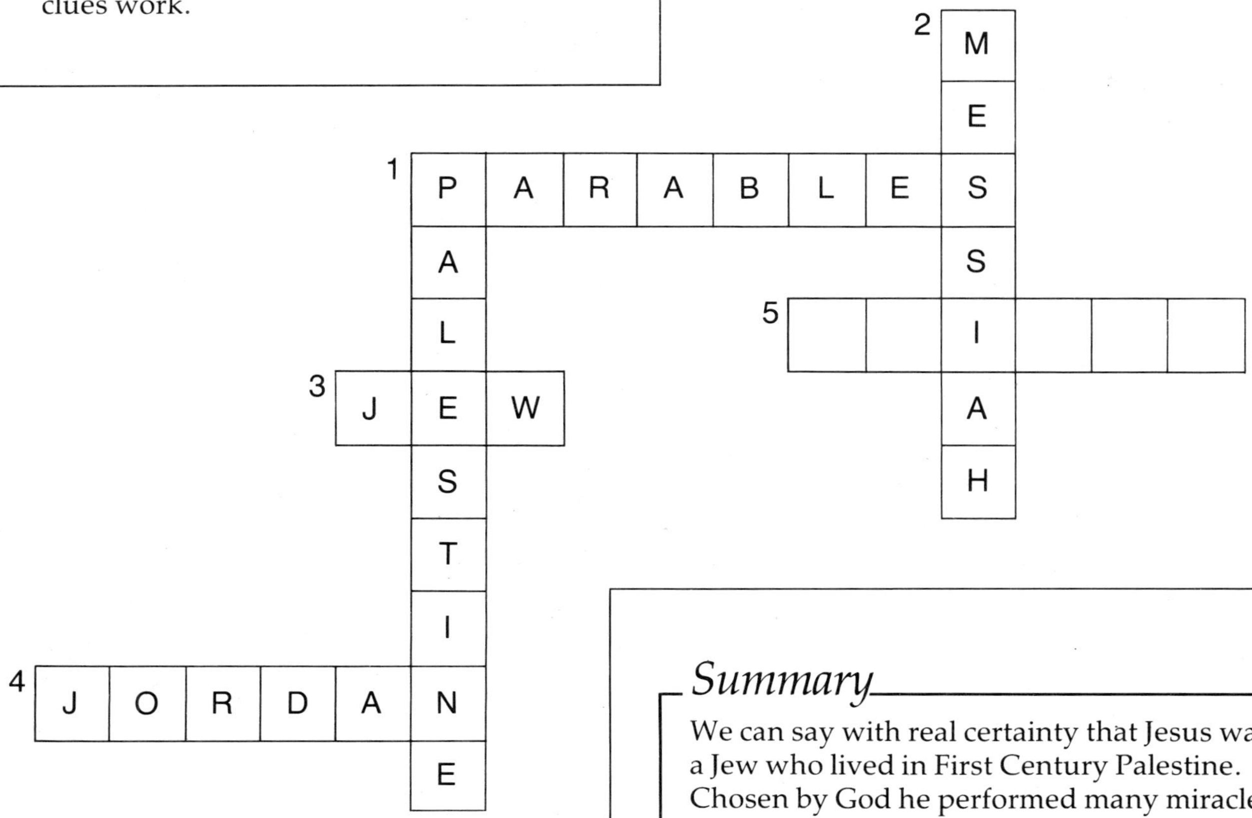

												2 M			
												E			
					1 P	A	R	A	B	L	E	S			
					A							S			
					L					5		I			
				3 J	E	W						A			
					S							H			
					T										
					I										
4 J	O	R	D	A	N										
					E										

Summary

We can say with real certainty that Jesus was a Jew who lived in First Century Palestine. Chosen by God he performed many miracles and taught the people using stories. He was rejected by the religious leaders.

3.3 *Jesus was a Jew*

A *'Finding Jesus in the Temple' painted by Holman Hunt, a nineteenth century English artist*

Jesus was born to Jewish parents and brought up within the traditions of that faith. As a young child, forty days after his birth, he was presented to God in the **Temple** which stood in Jerusalem. Of course before this he had been **Circumcised** on the eighth day of his life as all Jewish boys still are today.

When he was twelve years old a Jewish boy underwent preparation for his adult status as a member of the Jewish community. As part of this preparation Jesus was taken by his parents to the Temple during the great Passover festival. It was on this occasion that Jesus stayed behind in the Temple and astonished the learned rabbis and doctors by how much he knew (**A**).

When Jesus started to preach he began in the Jewish synagogue. It was only when the Jewish authorities tried to stop him that he moved out into the open air. From this time onwards the authorities began to plot against him. Eventually they were able to organize his death. But Jesus always showed that he was proud to be a Jew.

No group of Jews took themselves more seriously at the time of Jesus than the **Pharisees**. They spent much time studying the Jewish Law and surrounding it with many rules to protect it. This made the everyday lives of the people a misery and it was over this, more than anything else, that the Pharisees disagreed with Jesus.

During the past 2000 years relationships between Christians and Jews have not been as happy as they could have been. The Christians have often held the Jews responsible for the death of Christ. It has only been in recent years that the two religions have grown closer together. After all, Jesus was a Jew and Christianity owes a tremendous debt to the Jewish faith.

Things to do

B *Wooden carving of the nativity (birth of Jesus), West Africa*

1 Complete each of the following sentences with the most suitable word chosen from the column below:

a On the eighth day Jesus was...
b At the age of twelve Jesus was taken by his parents to the...
c The temple stood in the city of...
d Jesus began to preach in the...
e Then he began to preach in the open air because of the opposition of...

Jerusalem Synagogue
Circumcised Temple
Religious authorities

2 Write down a phrase or word which best suits each of the following descriptions:

i One of the religious groups which were most opposed to Jesus.
ii A building which stood in Jerusalem.
iii A religious practice carried out in the time of Jesus and still performed by Jews today.
iv A religious festival held in Jerusalem and visited by Jesus and his parents.

3 Look at picture **B**. Apart from Mary, Joseph and baby Jesus who do you think are the other characters in the carving?

4 Look up these references in the Gospels for yourself. What were the main reasons why Jesus argued with the religious authorities?

Mark 11.15–19
Matthew 15.1–9
Luke 6.1–5
Luke 7.36–50

Summary

Jesus was brought up in the Jewish tradition and at no time did he turn his back on it. It was only after a series of disagreements with the religious authorities that he began to preach in the open air instead of the Jewish synagogues.

3.4 *What did Jesus say?*

Jesus taught the people mainly by using parables. A parable was a story which was often like a riddle and you had to think hard about it to understand what it meant.

Matthew gathered many of these parables with snippets from the teaching of Jesus into the Sermon on the Mount (Chapters 5–7). Here Jesus encourages his followers not to make an outward show of their devotion to God. Those who do so are called hypocrites (people who pretend to be something they are not). Other men may admire them but God does not.

Whether a person is doing a kind act for someone else or praying to God it should be done in private. A person should give generously to others without counting the cost to himself. In this way he will receive God's reward. Jesus pointed this out one day when he was watching a widow putting her two small coins into the Temple treasury (Mark 12.41–44).

In telling these parables Jesus made use of many of the things that he saw around him. You can see two of these in pictures **A** and **C**.

B *'The prodigal son in the arms of his father' by G. Doré*

Many of the parables that Jesus told were about the character of God. He was just like the shepherd who leaves his flock and looks for the one sheep which has lost its way. God is the loving Father who cares for his children as in the story of the son who spends all his money and returns home penniless (Luke 15.11–32, see picture **B**).

Most of the parables were concerned with the Kingdom which Jesus came to set up on earth. The people were told that if they wanted to enter this Kingdom then they must be prepared to do two things: give up all that they had and follow the pathway set down by Jesus.

Jesus described all those who had already entered God's Kingdom as salt and light. Without salt food goes bad quickly and without light there is only darkness.

A *Painting of the parable of the wicked tenants. Read the complete story in Matthew 21.33-42*

Things to do

1 Prayer has always played an important part in the Christian religion. Jesus taught his followers to trust in God as their father and to speak to him naturally through prayer. Here is a modern translation of the Lord's Prayer which Jesus taught to his disciples:

> Our father in heaven;
> May your holy name be honoured;
> May your Kingdom come;
> May your will be done on earth as it is in heaven.
> Give us today the food we need.
> Forgive us the wrongs that others have done to us.
> Do not bring us to hard testing but keep us safe from the Evil One.

It has been pointed out that this prayer contains the four basic elements of all praying:

- praise to God
- the confession of sins
- praying for others
- praying for oneself

Which phrases in the prayer relate to each of these four elements?

C *Engraving of the parable of the sower*

2 Most of the parables of Jesus were drawn from real life. Here is one of the shorter ones:

'You are like a light for the whole world. A city built on a hill cannot be hidden. No one lights a lamp and puts it under a bowl.'

a In this parable who is like 'a light for the whole world'?
b Why is it pointless to hide a lamp under a bowl?
c Explain what Jesus was trying to teach people in this parable.

3 Here is a much longer parable. As you can see from picture **C** it, too, was based upon a common event in Palestine. Jesus used the parable to show the different ways in which people responded to his teaching.

Once there was a man who went out to sow corn. As he scattered the seed in the field, some of it fell along the path, and the birds came and ate it all up. Some of it fell on rocky ground, where there was little soil. The seeds soon sprouted because the soil wasn't deep. But when the sun came up it burnt the young plants; and because the roots had not grown deep enough, the plants soon dried up. Some of the seed fell among thorn bushes, which grew up and choked the plants. But some fell in good soil, and the plants produced a hundred grams, others sixty, others thirty.

a In this parable there are four kinds of soil. What are they?
b Read Mark 4.13–20 to see how Jesus applied the parable to his hearers. In your own words write down how Jesus used this story to teach people.
c Why do you think Jesus taught people through parables or stories?

Summary

Jesus taught people mainly by using parables or stories. Using the things around him Jesus told stories to show what God is like, how people can enter God's Kingdom and how they should live as Christians in God's world.

3.5 What did Jesus do?

A *Jesus walks on the water. Detail from bronze doors in Florence, Italy*

B *Jesus raises Jairus's daughter, from a fifteenth century Italian Bible*

At the beginning of his work Jesus was greeted enthusiastically by the people wherever he went. He chose twelve **disciples**, or followers, who would be taught by him and who would continue his work after he left the earth. Amongst his disciples were **Simon Peter**, who was later to deny that he had ever known Jesus, and **Judas Iscariot**, who was to betray him.

During the three years of his public work the Gospels tell us that Jesus did many remarkable things. They claim that among other things he:

- gave sight to the blind
- restored the power of speech to the dumb
- healed many lepers
- healed a paralysed man.

Furthermore we are told that he:

- brought three people back from the dead (**C**)
- calmed a raging storm
- walked on water without sinking (**A**)
- fed a large crowd with almost no food

These events are called **miracles**. There are many more of them recorded in the Gospels. Sometimes Jesus healed a person because he was very upset at his condition (**B**). Often he showed his power over nature to demonstrate to his disciples that he was God's son. Sometimes he used a miracle to test the faith of a person or that of his friends.

But the miracles are not the only things recorded about Jesus in the Gospels. Apart from teaching his disciples and the crowds of people who flocked to hear him Jesus also spent much time arguing with the religious leaders. He felt that they had made it more difficult for people to have faith in God. They would not accept his authority and sometimes his arguments with them were bitter and angry.

Quite apart from his public work we also know that Jesus often withdrew to one of the desert areas in Palestine. There he spent much time, often whole nights, praying secretly to God.

Things to do

1 Copy this crossword into your book and fill in the answers.

1 Name of the disciple who betrayed Jesus.
2 Name of another disciple of Jesus.
3 Jesus restored speech to the ________ man.
4 One kind of person that Jesus healed.
5 Jesus calmed a ________ storm.

2 **a** Look at pictures **A**, **B** and **C** again. In a few sentences describe the miracle which each picture shows.
b Why did Jesus use miracles?

3 Some people say that miracles do not take place any longer whilst others say that they never did. There are those people who say that miracles are impossible. Also you will find many people who claim that miracles do still happen if you look for them carefully enough.

a Collect any newspaper articles or information from television programmes which might suggest that a miracle has taken place. Talk about them with your friends. Do you think that they are describing a miraculous event?

4 You will find the story of a miracle in Luke 7.1–10. Read it through carefully and notice two unusual features about this particular miracle. First the man whose servant was ill was a Roman centurion. Secondly Jesus finds the faith of this man remarkable and far greater than that which the religious leaders had shown.

a Why was the Roman centurion worried about his servant?
b Why were some Jewish leaders concerned that Jesus should help this man and his servant?
c What were the two reasons why the centurion sent friends to stop Jesus on the way?
d Why was Jesus particularly impressed by the faith of this man?
e Imagine that you had been one of the crowd walking with Jesus. Write up an entry for your diary describing just what you saw and heard.

C *Lazarus walks out of his tomb, a nineteenth century engraving*

Summary

After choosing twelve disciples Jesus launched into his public work for the next three years. During this time he performed many miracles which showed his mastery over illness and the forces of nature.

3.6 *Jesus is put to death*

For some time the opposition forces had been grouping against Jesus. For once all of the religious leaders were in agreement. Jesus must be arrested, tried and put to death before he could have any more influence on the people.

So it was that Jesus, after living a public life for only three years, was arrested by the Temple Guards in the Garden of Gethsemane. He was first taken to the house of the Jewish High Priest to stand trial. The High Priest asked him a direct question:

> *Are you the Christ, the Son of the Blessed?*
>
> to which Jesus replied:
>
> *I am*

From there he was taken to the palace of Pontius Pilate, the Roman Governor. Pilate was most reluctant to condemn Jesus. He wanted to whip him and let him go. Pilate asked Jesus a direct question:

> *Are you the King of the Jews?*
>
> Jesus answered simply:
>
> *The words are yours.*

With the crowd demanding the death of Jesus Pilate condemned him and in exchange released Barabbas, a murderer. Jesus was handed over to the soldiers and dressed in royal purple with a crown of thorns on his head. The cane with which he was beaten was meant to represent a royal *sceptre* (the sign of a king). So Jesus was crucified (see picture **A**). As was usual a notice was nailed to the cross to show his crime. It said:

> *Jesus of Nazareth, King of the Jews.*

Both the Jews and the Romans were satisfied, for their own particular reasons, that Jesus deserved to die. For the first time in his life Jesus felt deserted by everyone, including God. Death by crucifixion usually took a long time but within six hours Jesus was dead. The last recorded words on his lips were amongst his best known:

> *It is finished.*

A *Painting of Jesus on the cross. Pictures* **B**, **C** *and* **D** *are also from the same series painted in the Middle Ages*

Things to do

B *Jesus falling under the weight of the cross and being beaten by a guard*

C *Jesus carrying the cross, with arm outstretched to Mary*

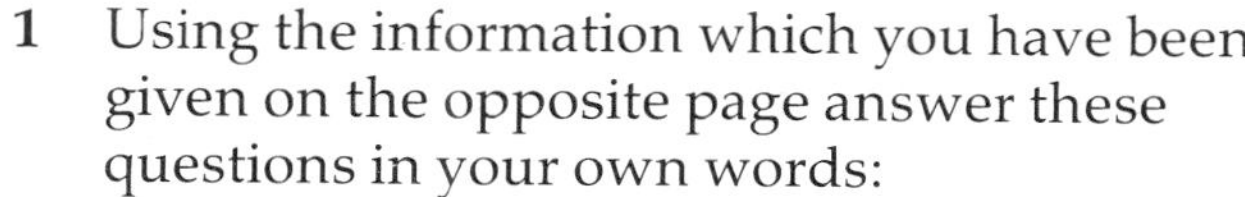

1 Using the information which you have been given on the opposite page answer these questions in your own words:

- **a** Where was Jesus praying when he was arrested by the Temple Guards?
- **b** Who was the Roman Governor who tried Jesus?
- **c** On what grounds did the Roman Governor condemn Jesus to death?
- **d** What happened to Jesus before he was executed?
- **e** What was unusual about the length of time that it took Jesus to die?
- **f** What did the notice nailed above Jesus on the cross say?
- **g** What were the last recorded words on the lips of Jesus?

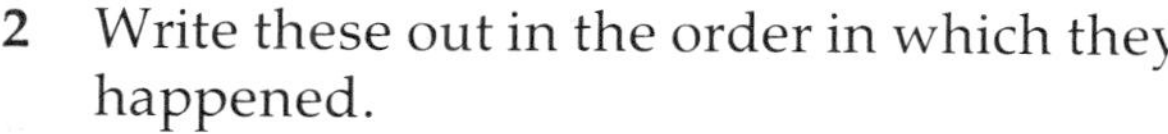

2 Write these out in the order in which they happened.

- **a** Jesus was mocked.
- **b** Pontius Pilate condemned Jesus.
- **c** Jesus was crucified.
- **d** Jesus was arrested.
- **e** Jesus was taken to the Jewish High Priest.

3 Each of pictures **B**, **C** and **D** show something that happened to Jesus between the end of his trial and his death. Describe in a few sentences what is happening in each of these pictures.

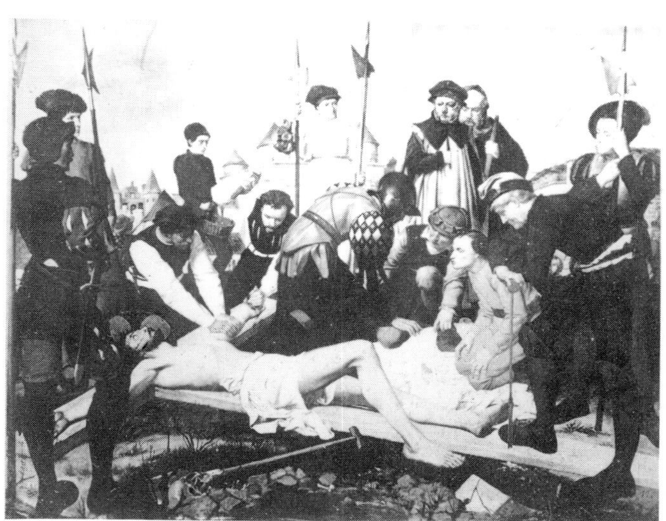

D *Jesus being nailed to the cross*

4 Each of the four Gospels describes the trial and death of Jesus. You can read one of them in Luke 22.47 – 23.56.

- **a** Imagine that you had been an eyewitness at the events that you have just read about. Describe them in your own words from the point of view of one of the people in the crowd in pictures **B**, **C** and **D**.

Summary

After his arrest Jesus was taken before the High Priest and then Pontius Pilate. It was Pilate alone who had the power to condemn him to death. After he had done so Jesus was whipped and then nailed to the cross in the early morning. By mid-afternoon he was dead.

3.7 *Jesus – after death*

A *Painting of the Resurrection by the school of Raphael*

In the time of Jesus wealthy people were able to afford special tombs in which they were to be buried with their family. These tombs were usually carved out of the hillside. Through the rolling stone door (see picture **B**) there was a stairway which led to an underground burial chamber. Another low opening led into a second chamber.

As soon as Jesus had died an important Jewish leader, Joseph of Arimathea, went to Pilate and asked for permission to lay the body in his own tomb. Having checked that Jesus was dead Pilate gave the necessary authority. As the Sabbath day had almost begun and no work was allowed the body was hurriedly wrapped in a cloth and laid on a ledge in the tomb.

On the day after the Sabbath, a Sunday, the women followers of Jesus went to the tomb to anoint (put ointment on) the body properly. This was always a woman's job in Palestine. They found that the tomb was empty. Instead two men dressed in white clothes told them:

He is not here; He has been raised.

The women were terrified and ran away.

B *Artist's impression of the garden tomb*

Later the women told the disciples of Jesus what they had seen. The Gospels tell us that Peter and John ran to the tomb to see for themselves. The tomb was empty. John noticed that the cloth and head covering had not been disturbed. He believed at once that Jesus had come back to life but Peter took more convincing. In the days that followed Jesus appeared to his disciples more than once and left none of them in any doubt that he was alive.

Christians believe that Jesus died to save all sinners. When he came back to life again this showed God's love for all people. The **Resurrection** of Jesus is celebrated each year by Christians on Easter Sunday.

Things to do

C *Mosaic of the 'risen' Christ*

1 a Why do you think the women were frightened and ran away from the tomb?
  b Why did Jesus appear many times to his disciples?
  c When do Christians celebrate the Resurrection?

2 Explain the following:

  a anoint
  b tomb
  c the Resurrection
  d Easter Sunday

3 Was the Resurrection the end of the story? You can piece the rest of it together for yourself by looking up these references:

  Matthew 28.16–20
  Luke 24.50–53
  Acts 1.6–11

4 Each of the Gospels contains its own account of the Resurrection of Jesus. Although they do not always agree on detail the broad outline of each story is the same. Read the account in Luke 24. carefully.

  Imagine you are one of the characters in the story writing your own life history at the end of your life. Write the chapter about the Resurrection of Jesus mentioning not only the details of the event but also the effect that it had upon you.

5 Picture **D** shows badges which carry messages about Christianity. Write down some reasons why you think a person might want to wear these badges.

D *Some badges often worn by young Christians*

6 Look at picture **A** again.

  a What do you think the guards are feeling?
  b How do you know the guards feel like this?
  c What is Jesus showing on his right hand?
  d The artist wanted to make this painting powerful. What can you see in the picture which makes it powerful?

Summary

After the body of Jesus had been lain in the tomb his women followers came to anoint it. They found the tomb empty and the body gone. Jesus was alive. He appeared to his disciples more than once. This event is known as the Resurrection.

4.1 *A place for worship*

Wherever you look you will find an impressive religious building – Westminster Abbey and York Minster in Great Britain; the Sikh Golden Temple at Amritsar in India; the Prophet Muhammed's Mosque in Medina in Saudi Arabia. Many of the world's most beautiful buildings are dedicated to the worship of God.

Yet we must remind ourselves that men and women worshipped God long before they put up special buildings for that purpose. For example, for some 300 years after the death of Jesus his followers met together in each others' homes for worship. When Moses led the Jews out of slavery in Egypt and through the desert the building of the first **Synagogue** was still hundreds of years away.

Religious buildings became necessary after some time in each religion so that worshippers could come together in large numbers to pray and praise. Over the centuries the size and shape of these buildings has varied considerably but you can usually identify a place of worship when you see one.

Each of these places of worship, whatever the religion, is believed to be holy ground. To show this a worshipper might wash or cross himself, bow, cover his head or remove his shoes. It all depends on whether he or she is entering a church (**A**), synagogue (**B**), mosque (**F**), mandir (Hindu temple) (**D**) or gurdwara (**E**).

A *Christian church in background*

B *Jewish synagogue in London*

Inside most places of worship there is a central point which attracts the attention of the worshipper. In a church it is often the **Altar** whilst in a synagogue it is the **Ark** in which the scrolls of the Holy Scriptures are kept.

Quite apart from being buildings in which acts of religious worship take place such places are also important because they act as meeting places for the people. Often, as with the synagogue and gurdwara, they also serve the people socially as various clubs and societies meet there.

C *Symbols of religions*

Things to do

D *Hindu mandir*

E *Sikh gurdwara in Bradford*

F *Muslim mosque in London*

1 Pictures **A**, **B**, **D**, **E** and **F** show different places of worship.

- **a** Can you see anything which the buildings have in common with each other?
- **b** Look at the symbols in picture **C**. Which symbols can you see on the outside of these buildings?

2 An old Hindu religious text tells us that:

The best places of worship are holy grounds, river banks, caves, sites of pilgrimages, the summits of mountains, confluences of rivers, sacred forests, solitary groves, the shade of the bel tree, valleys, places overgrowth with tulsi plants, pasture lands, cow sheds, island sanctuaries, the shore of the sea, one's own house, the abode of one's teacher, places which tend to inspire single-pointedness, lonely places free from animals.

- **a** What is this text trying to say about the best places in which to worship God?
- **b** Why do you think that the summits of mountains, overgrown places and the shores of the sea are good places in which to worship?
- **c** What do you think is meant by 'places which tend to inspire single-pointedness, lonely places free from animals'?

3
- **a** Are there any places which make you aware of the presence of God?
- **b** If so, where?
- **c** Why do they make you feel like that?

4 Look at picture **C** again.

- **a** What is a symbol?
- **b** Why do you think some religions have symbols?
- **c** Why do religious buildings often have their symbol on the outside of the building?
- **d** Copy the five symbols into your book and write under each one which religion it belongs to.

Summary

Although most religions started by worshipping God out of doors they all began to build their own places of worship. These buildings allow worshippers to pray and praise quietly and privately. The inside of each building is believed to be holy ground and those who enter it are expected to act respectfully.

4.2 The church

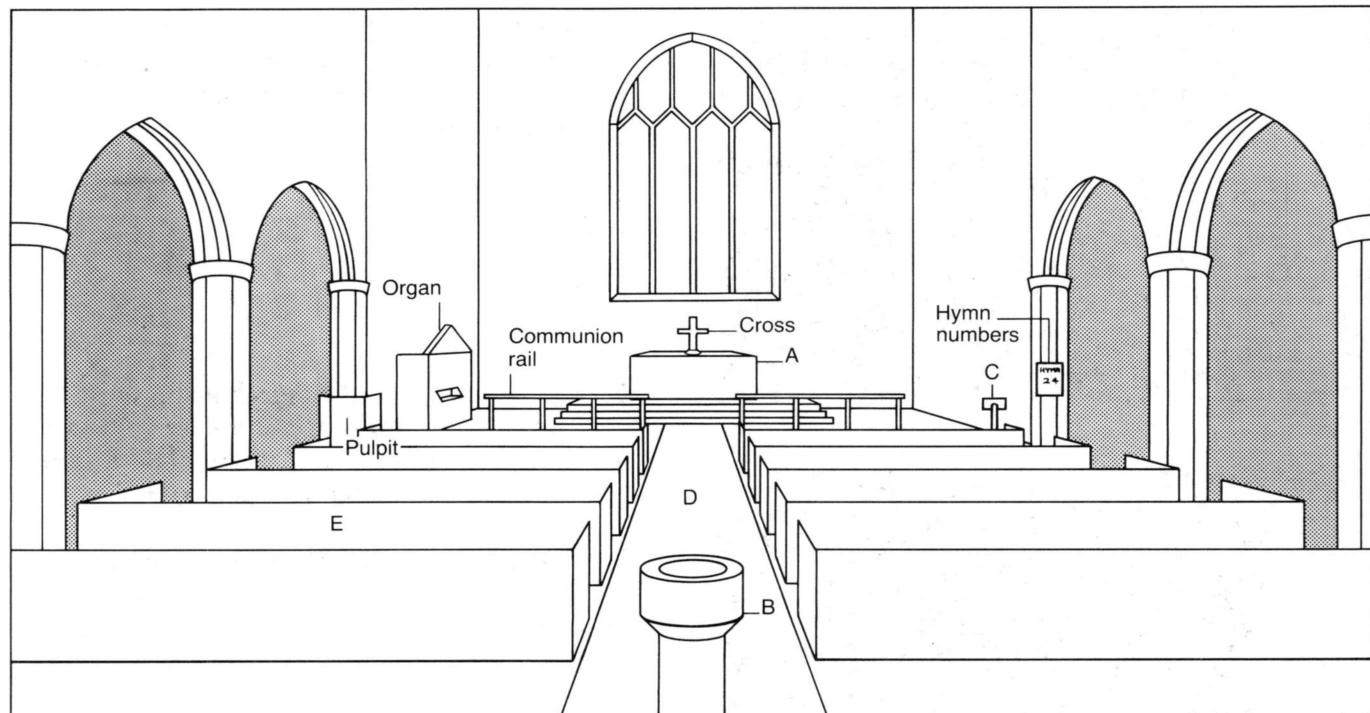

A *Plan of a church*

B *Bookshop at the back of a church*

For some 300 years after the death of Jesus Christ Christians met together in one another's homes. It was only when there were too many of them to do this that they began to build churches.

Many of the churches in this country are **Anglican** or **Church of England**. The most important of these buildings are **Cathedrals** each of which has a **Bishop** in charge. **Roman Catholics** also have their own cathedrals, churches and bishops. **Non-Conformists** such as Baptists, Methodists and Salvation Army meet together in smaller **Chapels**.

Picture **A** shows the inside of an Anglican Church. The focal point of the building is the **Altar**. The word itself means 'high' and the altar is often raised above the rest of the church. This is the holiest place in the church. It is in front of the altar that the people kneel to receive Holy Communion.

The *chancel* separates the altar from the choir stalls. The *lectern*, from which passages of the Bible are read, and the *pulpit* stand in the *nave*. The people sit in the *pews*. *Hassocks*, or cushions, hang along the back of the pews. People kneel on these when they pray. The idea of kneeling to pray probably comes from the custom of showing respect to a king. As God is believed to be greater than any earthly king so the Christian kneels in His presence.

Then inside the door of the church stands the *baptismal font*. This holds the water for baptism. Anglicans believe that a child becomes a member of the Church through baptism. It is for this reason that the font stands near the door to show that the child enters the Church through baptism.

Most of the churches in this country were built a long time ago. Many of those built recently serve as **Church Centres**. The majority of these have been put up on new housing estates. Here the church is often at the centre of the community life. Not only do people come to it to worship God but they also go there to relax, talk and discuss things with one another.

Things to do

C *Aerial view of a church*

D *Christian wedding*

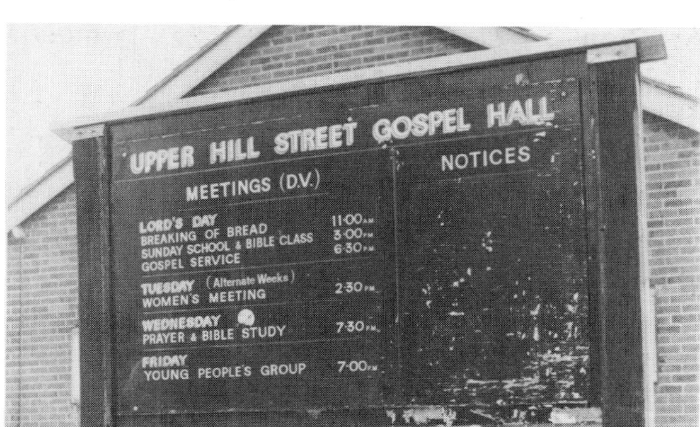

E *Noticeboard outside a Gospel Hall*

1 Look at the plan of the church in picture **A**. Using the information on the opposite page write down what happens at each of the places labelled.

a A
b B
c C
d D
e E

2 Picture **E** is of a church noticeboard. As you can see, it is very crowded and there seems a lot going on. Make a list of all the activities in which this particular church is engaged.

3 Look at pictures **B** and **D** showing different activities which go on inside churches. Describe what you think is happening and why.

4 Look at the view of a church from the air in picture **C** before going on to answer the questions below.

a In what shape was this particular church and many others like it built?
b Why do you think that this particular shape was chosen?
c Look at the other pictures on these two pages. Where else can you see this shape?

5 Imagine that a visitor from another country comes to your home. He asks about those buildings in the shape of a cross that he noticed as he was flying into the country. Describe to him the inside and outside of a church and explain what it is used for.

Here are some words to help you:

altar pews font nave
hymn numbers windows

Summary

As the cross is the symbol of the Christian religion many early churches were built in that shape. Inside an Anglican church the altar is the most important part.

4.3 *The synagogue*

Jewish people worship in a **synagogue**. The word itself means meeting place and that is just what happens in a synagogue. More than anything else it is a place in which Jews meet together to pray and to worship.

Inside the synagogue (see picture **A**), in the eastern wall facing the city of Jerusalem, there is a cupboard containing the scrolls on which are written the Holy Scriptures. This cupboard is called the **Ark**. The most important of the scrolls which it contains is the **Torah** (the Law) which is the first five books of the Jewish Bible (**E**).

Above the Ark in the synagogue the Ten Commandments can usually be seen written on tablets of stone. Normally these tablets show the first two words of each Commandment written in Hebrew (**D**). Apart from this and some other Hebrew letters there is no other form of decoration on the walls of the building.

In front of the Ark a light is always kept burning. This reminds Jewish people of the light which always burned in the old Temple hundreds of years ago. It also tells them that the scrolls kept in the Ark are very holy indeed.

In the centre of each synagogue there is a raised platform. Called the **bimah** this platform carries the reading desk from which long passages of the Torah and other books are read during the **Sabbath** morning service. In this way the Torah is read publicly from beginning to end throughout each year.

In most synagogues the men and women sit separately. By tradition Jewish people have always separated the sexes inside the synagogue for reasons of modesty. In the Medieval period special synagogues were built in some places so that women could conduct their own services.

B *Modern synagogue in London*

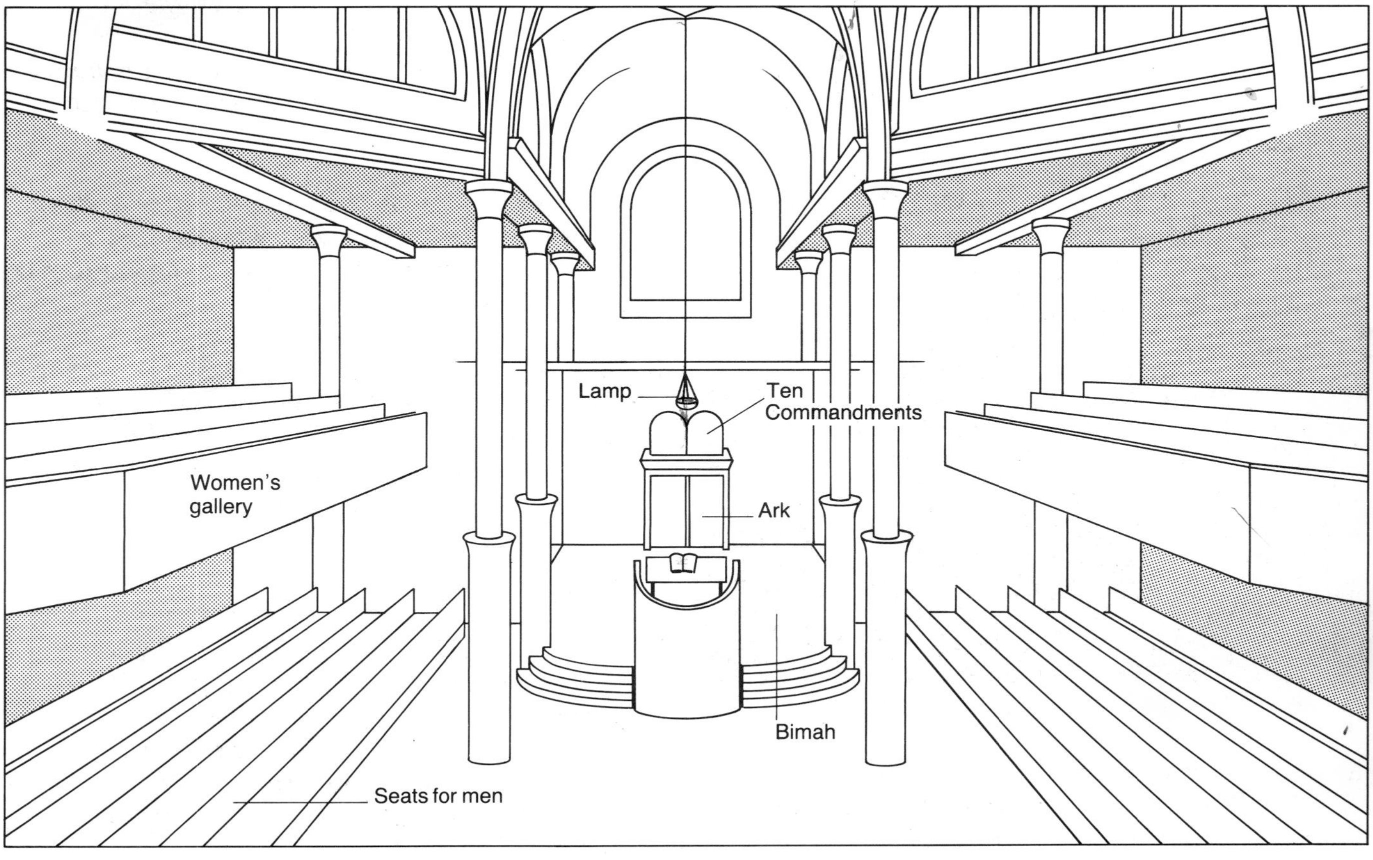

A *Plan of a synagogue*

Things to do

C *Service in Cricklewood synagogue, London*

1 Copy the plan of the synagogue into your book. Explain underneath the importance of each of the following:
  a The Ark.
  b The Torah.
  c The light which does not go out.
  d The women's gallery.

E *Rabbi holding the scroll of the law in front of the ark*

2 Look at picture **D**. Can you see that the first Commandment is written on the right not on the left. Why do you think these Commandments read from right to left?

D *The Ten Commandments*

3 **a** Why do people decorate the walls of their houses and buildings with pictures, paintings and posters?
  b Why do you think there are no decorations on the synagogue walls except for the Ten Commandments?

4 A modern guide to a synagogue says:

Visitors are often surprised at the apparent lack of formality in synagogue services . . . people may be seen talking to one another, entering and leaving the synagogue, and children play among the worshippers . . . there are certain parts of the service, when, provided the individual worshipper is not disturbed, his neighbours will talk to one another.

  a Is there a clue in the word synagogue itself to help you understand this quotation?
  b Why do you think that Jews like to worship like this?

5 Using the pictures on these two pages to help you, write a letter to a friend who has never seen a synagogue telling her what the building is like. Remember to describe both the inside and the outside.

Summary

A synagogue is a place where Jewish people come together, mainly to pray and study. It is also used for recreational purposes housing many Jewish clubs. The central point of any synagogue is the Ark. It is in here that the scrolls of the Jewish scriptures are kept.

4.4 The mosque

A *Outside Birmingham central mosque*

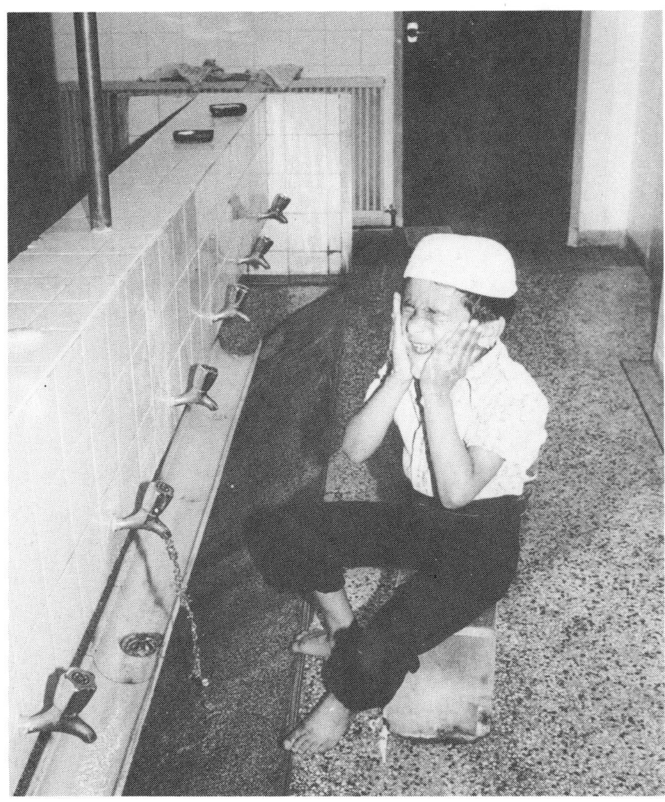

B *Muslim boy washing before prayer*

To build a **mosque** wins great merit for a Muslim in the sight of Allah (God). The Prophet Muhammed was believed to have said on one occasion:

He who builds a mosque for Allah's sake, Allah will build for him a house in Paradise.

Picture **A** is of Birmingham central mosque. Like all mosques throughout the world this one has been built facing the holy city of Mecca.

A mosque is the building in which Muslims pray. The word mosque means a place where a person bows down in the presence of God. It is also used for social gatherings, debates, lectures and weddings.

Each mosque is based upon the mosque which the Prophet Muhammed himself built in Quba, near to Medina. At one end of the building there is a courtyard. Here the worshipper washes himself very carefully before entering the building to pray (**B**). As he goes in he takes off his shoes and leaves them at the door.

Inside the building there are no seats. The room is almost bare and there are no pictures on the walls as these are strictly forbidden in the Qur'an. At one end of the mosque steps lead up to a small platform. It is from here that the **Imam** (leader of the mosque) delivers his sermon each Friday.

Above the mosque, as you can see from picture **A**, stands the dome and the **Minaret**. A minaret is a tower. It is from here that the call is given five times each day to call the faithful Muslim to prayer.

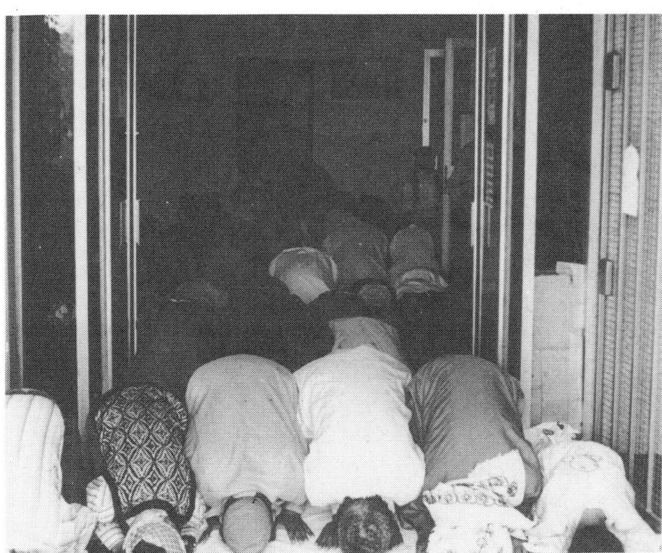

C *Muslims at prayer*

Things to do

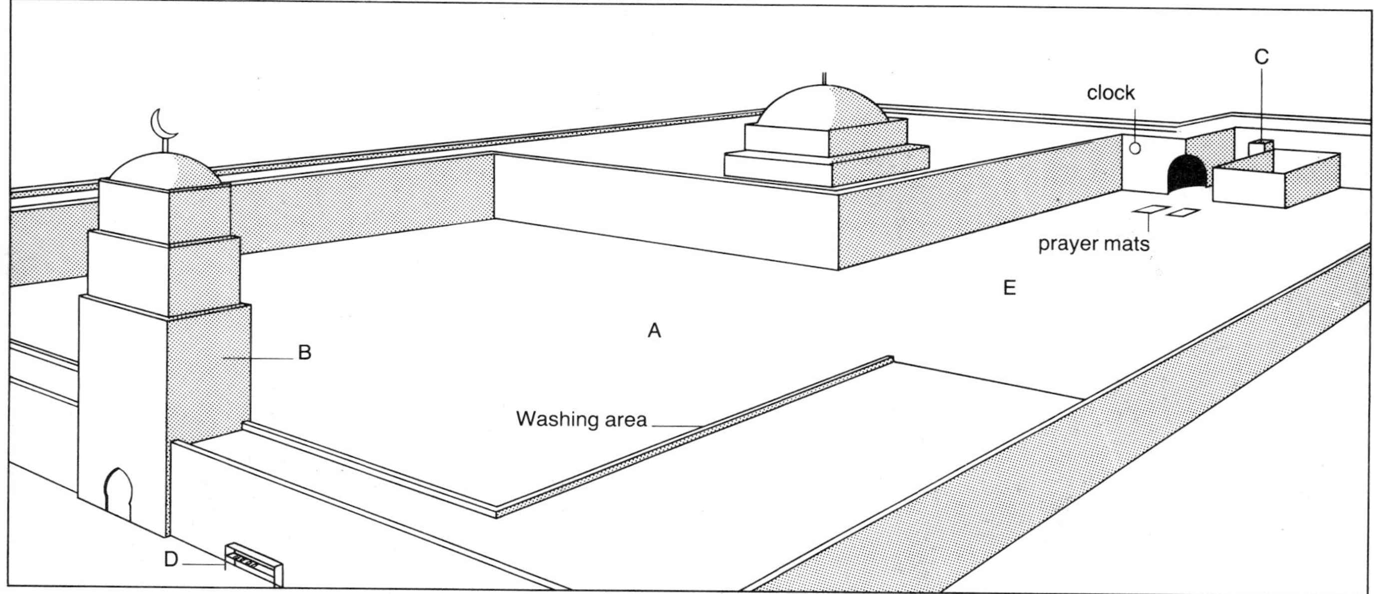

D *Plan of a mosque*

1 Look at the plan of a mosque in picture **D**. Write down what happens at each of the places labelled:
a A.
b B.
c C.
d D.
d E.

2 Look carefully at picture **A** of the mosque on the opposite page. Imagine that you came across this building in Birmingham by accident whilst you were walking around. How would you know from the outside that it was a mosque and not a church, synagogue, temple or gurdwara?

3 **a** Explain exactly what the Muslim worshipper is doing in picture **B**.
b Why do you think that washing is thought to be so important before entering a mosque to worship?
c Why do you think that all Muslims take off their shoes before entering a mosque?

4 The story is told about Muhammed that he taught his followers how important it is to wash before praying, to turn towards Mecca and to pray five times a day. A disciple asked him:

What if we cannot wash?

The reply came:

Wash yourself with sand.

And if we cannot find a clean place?

The questions went on. At last Muhammed said:

Even if you are not able to wash or clean yourselves, you do not know the direction of Mecca and you are not able to pray five times a day, nevertheless say your prayers when and where you can.

What do you think that Muhammed was trying to teach his followers about the mosque?

5 Using the pictures on these two pages to help you imagine you are one of the people in picture **A** walking into the mosque. Describe what you do before you start to pray and also what you can see around you in the mosque. Here are some words to help you:

remove shoes wash bare walls
Imam platform prayer mats

Summary

A mosque is a building in which Muslims gather for worship. The building, which always faces Mecca, may be beautiful or simply a house converted into a mosque.

4.5 *The gurdwara*

A *Raising the Sikh flag*

In recent years many **gurdwaras**, Sikh places of worship, have opened in this country. Above each gurdwara you will find the Sikh flag flying with its yellow background and black or blue symbols (see picture **A**).

As you enter the gurdwara there is a notice. It tells everyone who is about to enter that they must do three things before they go into the **Dewan Hall** (the prayer hall).

- Take off their shoes.
- Cover their head.
- Empty their pockets of all alcohol and cigarettes.

There are no seats inside the gurdwara. The worshippers all sit crosslegged on the well carpeted floor. There are two reasons for this. The first is that everyone must sit below the **Guru Granth Sahib**, the Sikh Holy Scriptures. The second reason is that everyone sitting on the same level emphasizes the Sikh belief that all people, both men and women, are equal.

As you can see from picture **B**, at one end of the gurdwara there is the **Takht** (the 'throne'). This is a raised platform on which the Guru Granth Sahib is placed. Any building which contains a copy of the Holy Book is considered to be a gurdwara.

The Granth is contained in beautifully embroidered covers. When the Book is not being read it is always covered. In some gurdwaras the Granth is placed in its own special room at night, and taken out each morning. Whenever the Holy Book is moved it is carried on the head.

Although the gurdwara is mainly a place where Sikhs can hear the reading of the Granth and say their prayers it is a social centre as well. In Great Britain the building is also used for teaching Sikh children and their parents the language of their homeland and the traditions of their religion (see picture **C**).

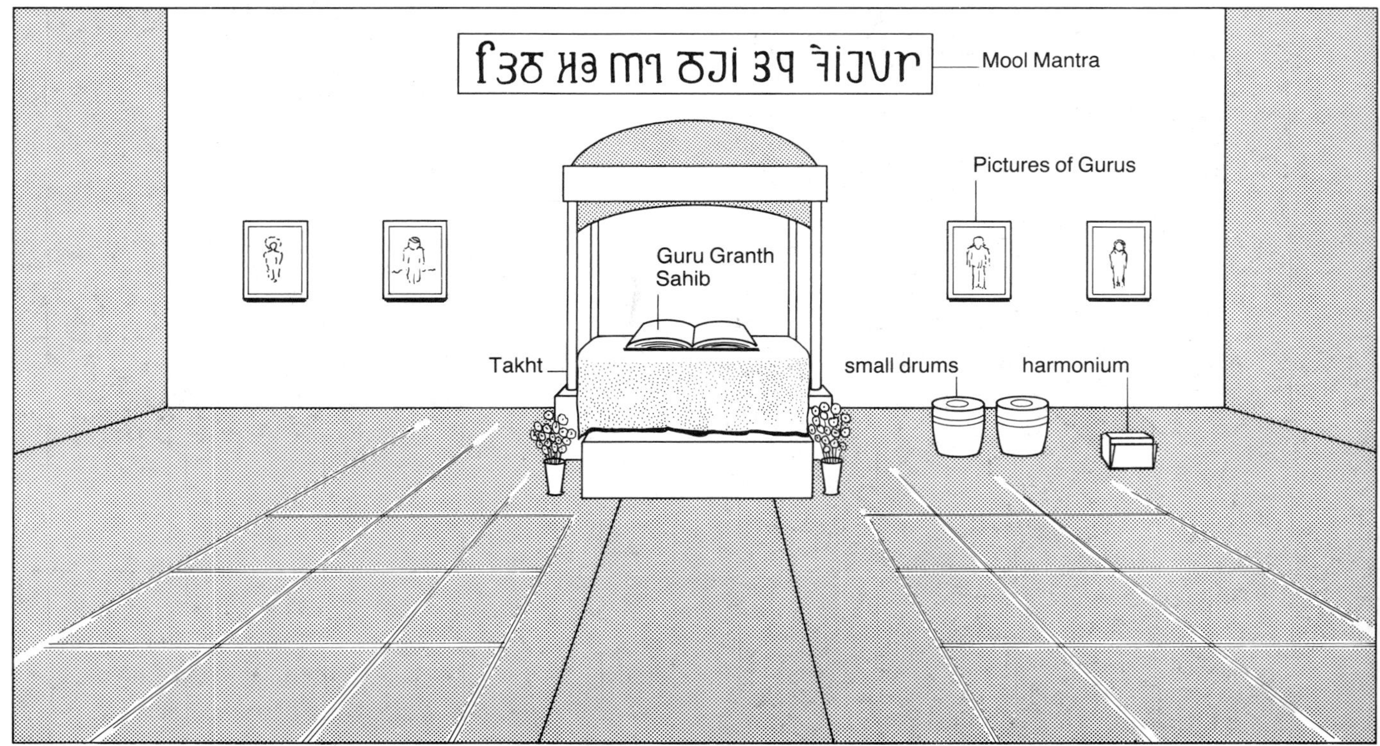

B *Plan of a Dewan Hall in a gurdwara*

Things to do

1 Each of these statements is either true or false. If true then copy them into your book as they stand. If false then copy in the correct version.

- **a** The Sikh flag flies above every gurdwara.
- **b** The Sikh flag is yellow with black or blue symbols.
- **c** Every Sikh must remove his shoes and cover his head before going into the gurdwara.
- **d** Sikhs are allowed to take alcohol and cigarettes into the gurdwara.
- **e** The Guru Granth Sahib is the Sikh Holy Book.
- **f** The Holy Book is given the central place in the gurdwara.

2 Here are some words which are used on the opposite page. Describe in a sentence what each of them means.

- **a** Gurdwara
- **b** Takht
- **c** Guru Granth Sahib

3 Imagine that you are responsible for taking a school party to visit a nearby gurdwara.

- **a** What instructions would you give the students before they entered the gurdwara?
- **b** What would you tell them to expect once they were inside the building?
- **c** Which central point in the building would you point out to the students?

C *Teaching in a gurdwara*

4 As picture **D** shows, many Sikh gurdwaras in this country are old churches which are no longer needed by Christians. Imagine that you are on a working party about to change a church into a gurdwara.

- **a** Describe what you might need to take out of the church and what you would put into the building.
- **b** How would you know that this particular building was a gurdwara and not a church?

5 Look at picture **C** again.

- **a** Why do you think these women are teaching the children Punjabi when they live in Great Britain?
- **b** Why is it important to learn the traditions of religion?

D *Group of Sikhs outside their temple*

Summary

A gurdwara is a Sikh place of worship. At the centre of the building is the Guru Granth Sahib, the Sikh Holy Book. This is treated with the greatest possible respect and is kept at one end of the building.

4.6 *The temple*

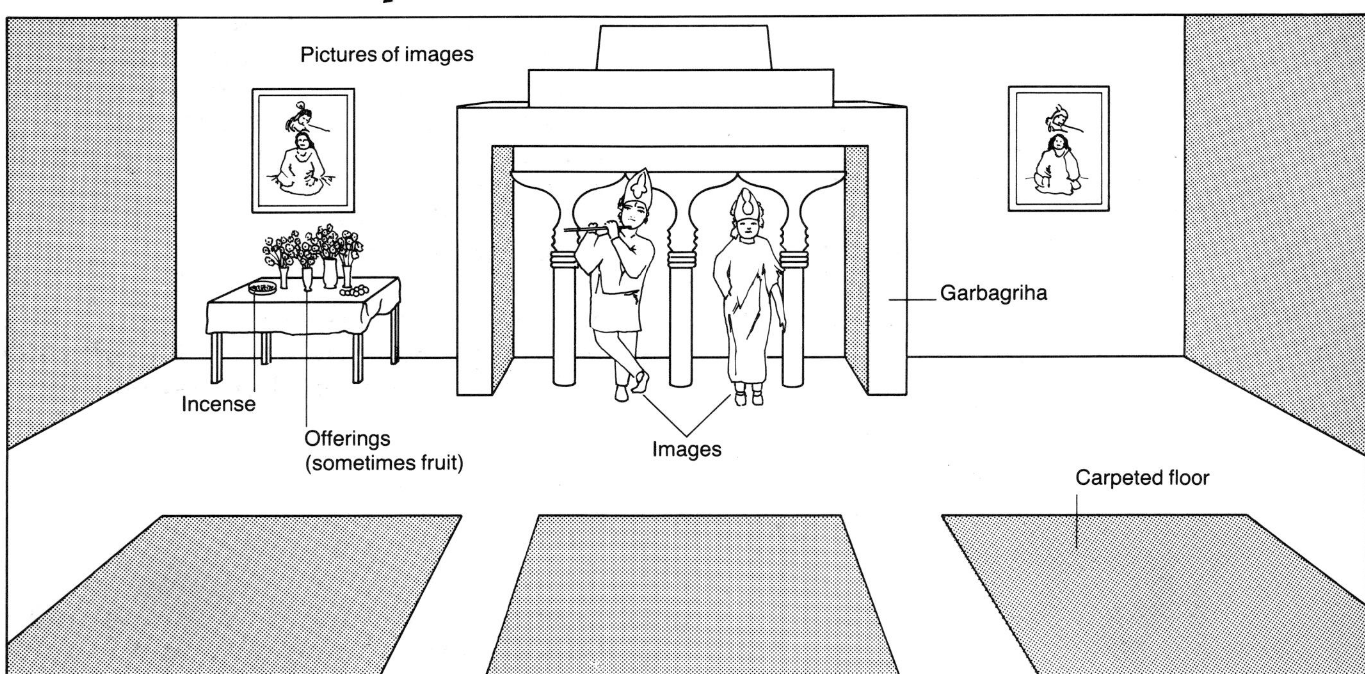

A *Plan of a temple*

Hindu **temples** come in all shapes and sizes. In Great Britain, where there are many Hindus, an ordinary house may be used as a temple. Purpose-built or not, if you step inside a Hindu temple you are likely to see that there is one main worshipping area (see picture **A**). As the worshippers enter this area they must remove their shoes. This is done as a mark of respect since they are standing on holy ground.

As in the mosque and gurdwara so in the temple there are no seats and the worshippers sit on the carpeted floor. Unlike these other two religious buildings the two sexes are allowed to sit together in a temple.

Inside each Hindu temple there is usually the very sweet smell of joss sticks being burned as **incense**. It is this smell which is believed to be very pleasing to the god. It also purifies the air.

At one end of the worshipping area you can find a statue of the god to whom the temple has been dedicated. In larger temples this statue is kept in the **garbagriha** (shrine room). The shrine room is usually kept shut. It is only the priest who is allowed to enter the room to wash and prepare the statue for worship. He does this once a week. At the same time he presents an offering of flowers, incense and fruit.

On special festival days the statue will be dressed in rich clothes and have a golden crown placed on its head. If the temple is not large enough to have its own priest then any responsible Hindu man can prepare the statue.

Many Hindu temples are dedicated to **Krishna**. According to Hindu belief he is the eighth form in which the god Vishnu visited the earth. Krishna is now a god in his own right.

B *Hindus carrying an image of the goddess Durga. She is their symbol of truth and bliss*

Things to do

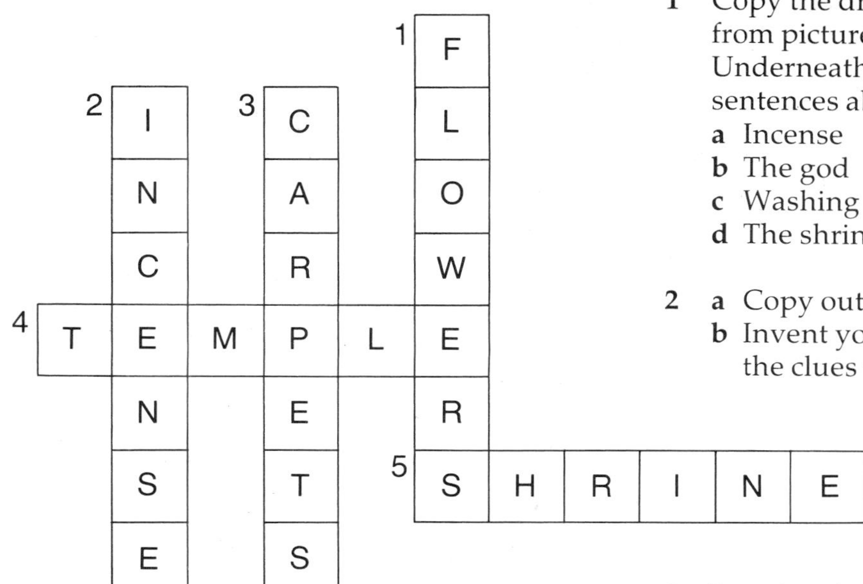

1 Copy the drawing of the inside of a temple from picture **A**. Label each item carefully. Underneath your drawing write two sentences about each of the following:

a Incense
b The god
c Washing the statue
d The shrine room

2 **a** Copy out this crossword.
b Invent your own clues for each word. Write the clues underneath the crossword.

3 Imagine that you have been invited to visit a Hindu temple by a friend of yours. Write a letter to your parents describing your visit and telling them everything you saw.

4 Compare and write down the similarities and differences of the five religious buildings you have read about in Unit 4. Here are some guidelines to help you:

- what do the buildings look like from the outside?
- what do the insides of the buildings look like?
- what do people do out of respect before they begin worship?
- where do people pray?
- what do people do inside the buildings when they are not praying?
- what are the central points of the buildings?

C *Hindu priest makes an offering to the gods in a house converted into a temple.*

Summary

Inside a temple there are no chairs and worshippers sit crosslegged on the floor. Joss sticks are burnt as incense. Each week the statue of the god is washed and specially prepared for worship.

5.1 *Christians at worship*

A *Service in a Baptist church*

B *Vicar giving wine at Holy Communion*

Worship is the practical way in which people express how they feel about God. As Christian belief centres mainly around Jesus Christ so his name frequently occurs in Christian worship. This is most clearly seen in the service of **Holy Communion**, which is the most important service in the Church of England (see picture **B**). In other Christian churches it is called the **Lord's Supper** or the **Breaking of Bread**.

In the hours before Jesus was crucified he ate a meal with his disciples. At this meal he broke bread and drank wine with his friends. At Holy Communion Christian worshippers do the same. This makes them aware of the death of Jesus which has given to them the forgiveness of their sins.

In the Christian Church an act of worship takes place when a group of believers come together to praise, honour and confess their sins to God. The singing of hymns, the reading of the Bible, praying and listening to the **sermon** are all parts of this worship. In this way those worshipping are not only seeking forgiveness for their past mistakes but are also looking to God for strength to live better lives in the future.

Picture **A** shows the **minister** leading Sunday morning worship in a **Baptist** church. You can see the hymn numbers displayed on a board at the front of the Church. You can also see the **pulpit** from which the minister delivers his sermon. In the sermon he explains a passage from the Bible to his congregation (group of religious worshippers).

C *Noticeboard in a church*

D *Children bringing gifts to the Harvest Festival service*

Things to do

E *Blessing the fields and crops*

F *Christening in a church*

1 Look at the pictures on these two pages showing Christian worship. Can you explain what is going on in each of the pictures?

2 What is the right word for these definitions?

- **a** A group of people who have come together to worship God in a Christian church. (a c________)
- **b** The practical way in which people express what they believe about God. (w________)
- **c** The most important Christian Service. (H________ C________)
- **d** The part of the church from which the sermon is delivered to the congregation. (p________)
- **e** The part of a service in which the minister explains a passage from the Bible to his congregation. (s________)

3 On the page opposite several reasons are given for Christians coming together to worship. What are they?

4 In this extract a young Christian is describing why the service of Holy Communion is so important to her personally.

In our church when we celebrate Holy Communion we are all remembering that the Lord Jesus Christ died, was buried and that he rose again from the dead three days later. To me the most important part is the belief that he rose again. This means that one day he will return to this earth again. Every time we celebrate Holy Communion we are being reminded of this fact.

- **a** Which three events does this young Christian remember every time that she celebrates Holy Communion?
- **b** What does she consider to be the most important part of Holy Communion?
- **c** What does she say that each Christian is looking forward to when he celebrates Holy Communion?

Summary

Each act of Christian worship includes praise, thanksgiving and sorrow for past sins. These different elements are expressed by singing hymns, praying and listening to the Bible being read. The Holy Communion is the central service of Christian worship.

5.2 *Jews at worship*

Saturday is the Jewish Sabbath and in the morning Jewish people make their way to the nearest synagogue. If at all possible they should walk rather than use a car or public transport. A complete service cannot be held unless a **minyan** (ten men) is present.

In most synagogues the men and women sit separately. The women take their places in the gallery and the men occupy the pews (seats) on the ground floor. Each man has his own seat for which he pays rent every year. As the service begins each person follows it in his **Siddur** (prayer book).

Each week a man is chosen to open the Ark. The scroll is then passed to the **Chazan** who carries it to the Bimah. It is a great honour then to be *called up* to give the reading of the Torah and say the blessings over the reading. After it is read the cover, crown and breastplate are replaced on the scroll before it is taken back to the Ark.

During the service psalms are sung from the Jewish Bible. As no musical instrument is allowed in most synagogues so each place has its own song-leader called a **Cantor**. Many prayers are also said during the service including the **Shema** and the **Amidah**. The Shema is taken from Deuteronomy 6.4 – 9 and is the basic statement of Jewish belief.

Hear, O Israel; the Lord our God, the Lord is one, And thou shalt love the Lord thy God with all thy heart and with all thy soul and with all thy might.

A *Reading the Torah at Yom Kippur, the holiest day in the Jewish calendar*

B *Mother and daughter with lighted candles at the beginning of the Sabbath, Friday evening*

C *Service for Jewish cubs and scouts*

Things to do

D *Purim is a time for parties and carnivals. When Haman (a man who wanted to massacre the Jews 2000 years ago) is mentioned everybody has to drown his name with noise*

1 Here are some words taken from the opposite page. Explain in just one sentence what they mean.
  - **a** A Minyan
  - **b** A Siddur
  - **c** The Bimah
  - **d** The Cantor
  - **e** The Shema

2 Copy into your book and learn the Shema off by heart. Then answer these questions:
  - **a** What does the Shema tell the people about God?
  - **b** What does it tell them that their response to God should be?
  - **c** Why do you think that the people are told to love God
    'with all thy heart, and with all thy soul and with all thy might' ?
  - **d** Explain underneath why the Shema is considered by Jews to be so important.

3 The scroll of the Torah is carried around the synagogue before it is read.
  - **a** Why do you think that it is carried above head height?

4 The Amidah prayer contains nineteen blessings. Here is just a brief extract:

O Lord, open thou my lips, and my mouth shall declare thy praise.
Blessed art thou, O Lord our God and God of our Fathers, God of Abraham, God of Isaac and God of Jacob, the great, mighty and revered God, the most high God who bestowest loving-kindnesses and possessest all things; who rememberest the pious deeds of the patriarchs and in love wilt bring a redeemer to their children's children for thy name's sake.

  - **a** Which three people from the Jewish Scriptures are described as the 'Fathers' of Jewish people?
  - **b** Make a list of all the things that this extract says about God.

Summary

The main Jewish worship of the week takes place in the synagogue on a Sabbath (Saturday) morning. Prayers, singing the Psalms and reading the Torah are very important elements in a Jewish act of worship.

5.3 *Muslims at worship*

A *The Iman leading prayers during a wedding service*

In Muslim countries the **Muezzin**, an official of the mosque, climbs to the top of the minaret five times a day to issue his call to prayer. In this country the call still goes out but is usually made inside the building. Wherever it is said, the words are always the same (see question **1** on the opposite page).

All male Muslims must attend the mosque for prayers at midday on Friday. Before entering the mosque they take off their shoes as a sign of respect for Allah. Most people wash at home first but others use the fountain or tap provided. Each person washes his hands, rinses his mouth and nostrils, washes his arms to the elbows, then lightly wipes over his forehead, ears and neck before finally washing his feet to the ankle. This procedure is repeated three times.

This washing is very important. Not only must the worshipper be spiritually clean as he enters the presence of Allah but physically clean as well.

Once he has washed and covered his head (another sign of respect) the worshipper enters the mosque to pray (**C**). The Prophet said that prayer is like a stream into which the faithful believer dives five times every day. Just as water cleanses the outside of a person's body so prayer cleanses his soul.

Each Friday the prayers are led by the **Imam**. He takes all of the worshippers through the **Rakah** (**A**). This is a sequence of twelve positions, at each of which the worshippers must stop to say different prayers. Twice during the Rakah he will end up face downwards to the ground. This represents respect and complete submission to Allah.

Muslim worship is almost totally a matter of prayer. In fact a Muslim can pray anywhere, providing it is in a clean place. When the Muslim is not in a mosque it is normal for him to use a **prayer mat** (see picture **B**). This must be in a plain colour. It must also contain the figure of an arch which is then pointed towards Mecca.

Muslim women must pray in the same way. They can do this in their own homes and do not need to come to the mosque.

B *Prayer mat*

Things to do

C *Muslims praying in a mosque*

1 The call to prayer is always issued by the muezzin in Arabic. Here is an English translation:

God is the greatest. God is the greatest. God is the greatest. God is the greatest.
I bear witness that there is no God but Allah. I bear witness that there is no God but Allah.
I bear witness that Muhammed is the messenger of Allah
I bear witness that Muhammed is the messenger of Allah.
Come to prayer. Come to prayer.
Come to security. Come to security.
God is the greatest. God is the greatest.
There is no God but Allah.

a What is the Muslim name for God?
b Who was God's Messenger?
c Where is the Muslim to go for prayer?
d Why do you think that each phrase is repeated at least twice?
e Which phrase is repeated six times?
f Why do think that this phrase is the most important?

2 Explain the following:
a prayer mat
b rakah
c muezzin

3 In picture **B** you can see the design for a prayer rug.
a Either copy this drawing into your book or, better still, design your own prayer mat. Remember that each prayer mat must contain the design of an arch which can be pointed towards Mecca.
b Underneath your drawing explain why a Muslim needs to use a prayer mat and when.

4 The main emphasis in Muslim worship is upon the greatness and mercy of God and the weakness and needs of man.
a How is this brought out in the Muslim attitude towards prayer?
b Compare the call to prayer with the Lord's Prayer (there is a modern version on p 31)
i Are the two prayers similar?
ii Do they approach God in a similar way?
iii What are the main differences?

Summary

A Muslim is called to prayer five times each day but the most important is the noonday prayer on Friday. He must carefully wash himself before he begins to pray. Once in the mosque he goes through the long sequence of the Rakah, adopting a different position to say each of the prayers.

5.4 *Sikhs at worship*

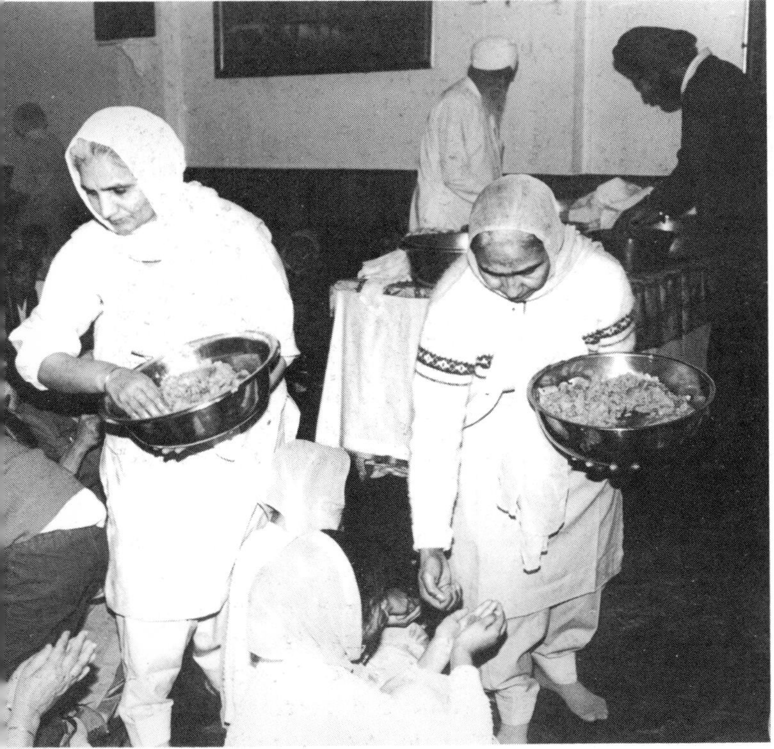

A *Giving out Karah Parshad*

As a worshipper enters the gurdwara he takes off his shoes as a sign of respect. Having bowed low he can also present his gift of food or money together with a silk cloth to cover the Granth if he wishes to do so.

Sikh men wear **turbans** to cover their heads and the women **dupattas** (see pictures **A** and **B**). These are silk or cotton scarves. A man's hair is the most important part of his faith and a turban is necessary to keep the hair in order. It is also a symbol of the Sikh faith.

Anyone, male or female, can conduct a Sikh service. The religion has no priests as everyone is considered to be equal. The service itself can last for any length of time between one and five hours. The worshippers come and go as they please.

During the service the Guru Granth Sahib is kept covered up unless someone is reading from it (**C**). The **Granthi** (religious teacher) sits behind the Holy Book throughout the service and waves a **chauri** over it. This is a yak hair or peacock feather fan. It shows the authority which the Holy Book is believed to have.

Meanwhile the congregation are sitting crosslegged on the floor. Men are on one side of the gurdwara and women on the other. Hymn singing is a very important part of a Sikh service and this is often accompanied by musicians using a harmonium and a pair of small drums (see picture **B**).

During the service everyone stands and facing the Granth Sahib sings the Common Prayer. This is called the **Ardas** and a short extract can be found in question **2** on the opposite page.

At the end of the service **Karah Parshad** is given to the congregation. It is a mixture of flour, sugar and clarified butter (called ghee). This is cooked in the gurdwara kitchen and brought into the hall before the close of the service. It is touched with a kirpan (sword) before distribution (**A**).

The fact that everyone eats together demonstrates that all people are equal and united in their faith. It is sweet-tasting to emphasize God's great kindness in his dealings with the human race. Karah Parshad also shows that no one is allowed to leave the Guru's presence empty handed.

After the service everyone gathers for the **Langar** (traditional meal) which is served elsewhere in the gurdwara. People sit in rows to eat, with the men and women still separate. The object of the meal is to bring together all members of the Sikh community and to break down any barriers that there might be between them (**D**).

B *Sikhs playing musical instruments*

Things to do

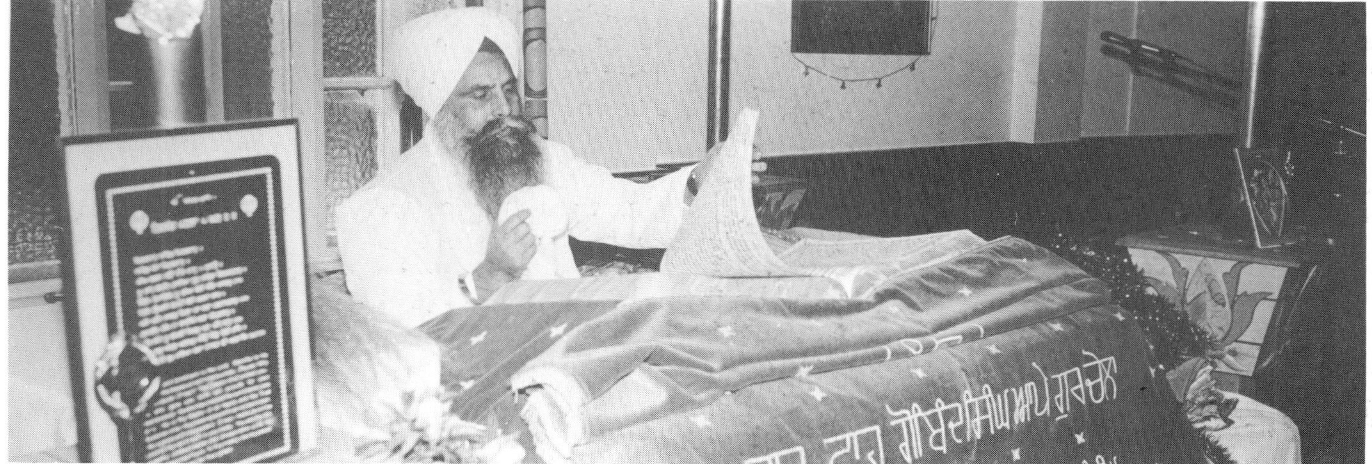

C *Reading from the Guru Granth Sahib*

1 People often share a meal with friends to celebrate a special occasion like a birthday or wedding.
   a Write down any other occasions you can think of when people eat a meal to celebrate something special.
   b Why do you think friends celebrate a special event by eating a meal together?
   c What religions do you know of which include a meal in their service?

2 Here is a short extract from the Ardas, the Sikh Common Prayer.

   O true king, O loved Father, we have sung Thy sweet hymns, heard Thy life-giving Word . . . may these things find a loving place in our hearts and serve to draw our souls towards Thee. Save us, O Father, from lust, wrath, greed, undue attachment and pride . . . Give us light, give us understanding, so that we may know what pleases Thee . . . Forgive us our sins . . . .

   a Which two names are applied to God?
   b What five things does the worshipper ask God to save him from?
   c What three things does the worshipper ask God to do for him?

3 Sikh people do not set aside a special day for worship although in this country most gurdwaras hold their services on a Sunday. Why do you think some religions think it is important to have one special day every week for worship and others don't?

4 Here is one Sikh describing his weekly visit to the gurdwara.

   Everyone starts by saying the hymns from our Holy Book and ends by joining in a special meal. As we worship God together our children are allowed to wander around freely just as they like. To be truthful there is a lot of movement throughout the service as people come and go all the time. We are used to this but visitors find that it is rather strange.

   The end of the service is the most important time and all of the worshippers are expected to be there for that.

   A Sikh service sounds a relaxed occasion.

   a Which kind of religious service would you most like to attend – one that was strictly organized or one that was far more casual?
   b Why?

D *The langar after the service*

Summary

The Sikh Holy Book is the centre of every act of worship. Throughout each service great respect is shown to the Granth. A Sikh service is very long and always ends with a meal.

5.5 *Hindus at worship*

There is no set time or place at which all Hindus are expected to come together to worship. Even when they do their worship does not take any fixed pattern except at festivals when priests follow set forms of prayer.

Worship begins at home for the Hindus. Each morning when they get up, usually early, Hindus will have a good bath. They cannot pray until their bodies are clean. Whilst they are washing they decide what form their prayers will take for that day.

That may involve a visit to the nearest temple. Here many worshippers gather in front of the shrine. Picture **D** shows the image of **Ganesha**, the elephant-headed son of **Parvati**.

Meanwhile the priest presents each worshipper with a blessed offering, **prasad**, which has been made from milk, sugar and ghee (melted butter). Sometimes the priest will also make a mark on the worshipper's forehead (see picture **B**).

B *Hindu wearing the stripes of Shiva on his forehead*

Acts of worship such as these can be repeated at any time. At the moment there are few Hindu temples in this country although some groups are now building their own temples or converting existing buildings.

Until quite recently no one was allowed to perform any Hindu act of worship outside India. This meant that Hindus living in this country had to rely on relatives at home to carry out such ceremonies on their behalf. Now there is no such restriction and Hindu acts of worship are carried out regularly in many of the large towns and cities of Britain.

A *Hindu priest blesses the statues of Lord Rama, Sita and Laxmana*

Things to do

C *Cooking in the temple kitchen*

1 Write out and complete the following sentences using the information on the opposite page.

a Ganesha is the ________-god in the Hindu religion and the son of ________.

b ________ and ________ are often presented as offerings to the Hindu gods.

c The priest presents each worshipper with a ________ which is also called a ________.

d One of the marks which the priest might place upon the worshipper's forehead is the ________ of Shiva.

e Before attending an act of worship in the temple each Hindu will ________ himself thoroughly.

2 Many Hindus in this country do not attend the temple regularly. Here is one young Hindu girl who lives over here with her family describing a visit which she had recently made back to India.

When I was in India a few weeks ago my parents took me to see many Hindu temples but I wasn't too sure what to make of them. My mum told me that if we still lived in India then we would visit the temple every day to say our prayers. That is the custom over there.

In this country, however, things are very different. We do not have a temple anywhere near to where we live and so we just pray to God wherever we might be – in the house or in the open air.

a Do you think that a young Hindu might find it difficult to practice her religion without going anywhere near a temple?

b What do you think would be the advantages for a Hindu in meeting other Hindus in a temple if that was possible?

3 Compare and write down the similarities and differences of worship in the five religions you have read about in Unit 5. Here are some guidelines to help you:

- when do they worship
- where do they worship
- what happens in their service
- do they have a religious leader and what does he do
- is there a meal in the service and what is it like

D *Ganesha*

Summary

Hindus worship both at home and also in the temple. Services in the temple can take place at any time. Sitting in front of the shrine of the god each worshipper is given a sweetmeat and usually has a mark placed upon his forehead by the priest.

6.1 *The Jewish Prophets*

A *Painting of Daniel in the lion's den*

A **prophet** was a man in early Jewish history who was believed to have been inspired by God. Sometimes he could foretell future events but he was usually there to speak critically to the people from God.

Probably the first Jewish prophet was Moses. His sister Miriam was known as a prophetess and so was another woman called Deborah (**C**).

Later on the prophets were to play a very important part in Jewish history. There was Amos, a herdsman by profession, who suddenly appeared in the market place and started preaching the Judgement of God. Another prophet, Hosea, told the people that they were like his own wife, faithless. They had been unfaithful to God just as his wife had been unfaithful to him.

Then followed a whole succession of prophets who told the nation of Israel that God would judge them. Isaiah declared that they were hypocrites since the people carried out all the religious rules but forgot to look after the poor and the helpless. When Jeremiah told the people a similar thing he was branded a traitor and put into prison (**D**).

Other prophets suffered too. Daniel was put into the lion's den because he refused to stop praying at the king's command. Like Jeremiah, Daniel survived because God was with him (**A**).

Although most of the prophets lived more than 2500 years ago they are not forgotten by Jews today. Apart from the Torah (the Law) no part of the Jewish Bible is more highly valued than the Prophets. Passages from it are read out regularly during synagogue services.

B *Wall carving of Jonah and the whale*

Things to do

C *Deborah, the prophetess*

D *Engraving of Jeremiah being set free*

1 Unscramble the words in brackets below and then copy out the complete sentences.
   - **a** Men who spoke on behalf of God to the Jewish people were called (THPOSERP)
   - **b** Probably the first Jewish prophet was (ESMOS)
   - **c** The prophet who likened Israel to his own faithless wife was (SOEHA)
   - **d** (BREADHO) was a prophetess
   - **e** (RJIAEMEH) was a prophet who ended up in prison
   - **f** (IAISAH) told the people that they neglected the needy and the helpless.

2 Here is an answered crossword. Copy it out. Under your copy write down clues for each word.

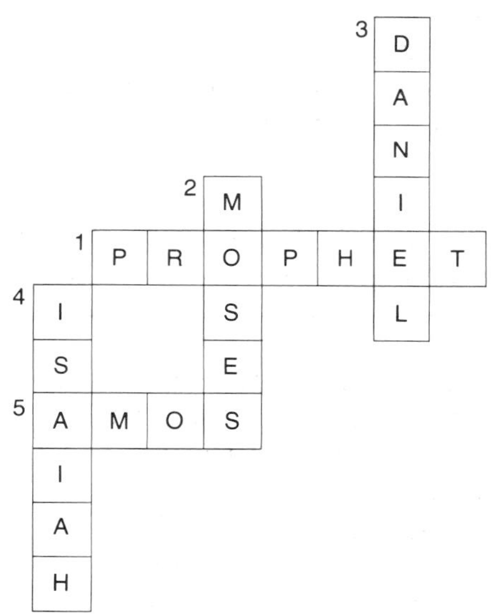

3 Imagine that a prophet, like one of those that you have read about, were to visit your country today.
   - **a** What kind of things do you think he would have to say?
   - **b** Are there any things that he would be very happy about?
   - **c** Which things do you think that he might be paticularly unhappy about?

   You could illustrate your answer with cuttings taken from newspaper and magazine articles. You might like to extend this into a wall display of the things which concerned the prophets of old and the things which concern people today.

4 Read Jonah 1.1 – 2.10 and look at picture **B**. Describe the events in Jonah's life which you can see in the carving.

Summary

The prophets were men in early Jewish history who spoke to the people on God's behalf. Not only did they look into the future but they criticized the way that people were living.

6.2 *The saints*

A *Twelfth century wall painting of St Paul*

B *Engraving of St Catherine*

A **saint** is a person in the Christian religion who has shown outstanding love for God and holiness in life. Often, although not always, a saint is a **martyr** (someone who has been put to death for his beliefs). After their death miracles are often associated with their burial places.

Many of the early saints were killed violently. Amongst the first to die were St Peter and St Paul who are believed to have died in the persecution in 64 CE led by the mad Roman Emperor, Nero.

After Polycarp was put to death in 155 CE his bones were collected by his followers and said to be 'more precious than jewels of great price'. The bones were buried in a safe place but dug up again when his disciples met to celebrate his death. In the case of a martyr, the **natalis** (death day) was always very important since this day was the birthday in heaven of the martyr, reunited with Christ by his death.

It soon became the custom to put the bones of a martyr under the altar in a church. This was thought to be the best place for a servant of Christ to end his days.

In the Middle Ages the **relics** (bones) of a saint were believed to bring healing. Hundreds of people travelled as pilgrims from shrine to shrine hoping to be cured.

The relics also protected the churches that housed them. Churches often competed against each other to own them. Large sums of money frequently changed hands.

Since then many of the most popular saints have been largely forgotten. Others still live on, for example in the names of our parish churches.

C *Woodcut of St Stephen being stoned*

Things to do

1 Copy out these sentences and fill the blanks from the words below:

altar Peter Polycarp Paul martyr burial places Nero natalis

a A ________ is someone who has laid down his life for his beliefs.
b After the death of a saint miracles were often associated with their ________.
c Both St ________ and St ________ were believed to have died at the hands of the mad Roman Emperor ________.
d The bones of St ________ were said to have been 'more precious than jewels of great price'.
e The death day of a martyr was known as the ________.
f The custom in the Middle Ages was to bury the bones of a saint under the ________ of a church.

2 Explain in your own words the meanings of:
a saint
b martyr
c natalis
d relics

3 Shortly before he was martyred St Polycarp was given an opportunity of turning his back upon the Christian faith. He is said to have replied:

For eighty-six years I have been his (Christ's) servant and he has never done me wrong; how can I blaspheme my king who saved me?

What do you think that Polycarp meant when he said this?

4 A modern writer describes the death of Polycarp in the following way:

When the crowd at the games in the amphitheatre was told that Polycarp had confessed that he was a Christian they shouted first for the lions and then for him to be burnt at the stake. He was bound; an official killed him with his sword; his body was then burnt.

a Imagine that you are St Polycarp. Write an account of the last few minutes of your life and the thoughts that are going through your mind at the time.

5 a Make a list of all the saints' names you can think of.
b Then write down as much as you can about three of the saints on your list.

D *An engraving of St Luke who is thought to have been a doctor*

Summary

A saint is a Christian who has shown outstanding love for God and has often shown this by sacrificing his life for his beliefs. From Peter and Paul onwards the list of saints is a long and distinguished one.

6.3 The Sikh Gurus

A *The Sikh Golden Temple at Amritsar, India*

Sikhs believe that whilst ordinary men continue to be reborn many times their **Gurus** (spiritual teachers) do not. Nanak was the first Guru and Gobind Singh (1666–1708) was the last.

Guru Nanak died in 1539. Neither of his two sons were fit to lead the Sikhs. Instead he chose one of his followers, Bhai Lehna, to succeed him and gave him the name **Angad** (my limb). Angad made the Punjabi language known to the common people so that they could understand the many hymns of Nanak.

When Guru Ram Das, who succeeded Angad, became leader, he insisted that every Sikh place of worship should have a kitchen attached (see picture **C**). Here the rich and the poor could be fed alongside one another. Guru Das also founded the city of Amritsar and thousands of people came to visit it.

The next Guru, Arjan, prepared the Holy Book, the Guru Granth Sahib, for all Sikhs to read. He also built the Holy Golden temple in Amritsar (see picture **A**). Amritsar soon became the centre of the Sikh Empire.

Arjan was also the first Guru to die for his faith. Burning sand was poured over his body by Turkish Muslims before he was made to sit in very hot water and then placed upon a red hot iron plate and roasted to death.

The seventh and eighth Gurus were able to live peaceful lives but the ninth, Guru Tegh Bahadur, was beheaded by the Muslim Emperor.

The tenth and final Guru was Gobind Singh. During his time the followers of Nanak were being persecuted. In 1699 Singh called all Sikhs together in Anandpur. With a drawn sword he asked them:

Is there anyone who will give up his head to prove his faith in me?

One man volunteered, went into the tent with Singh, there was a thud and blood poured out under the tent flap. This happened four more times but then all five men came out of the tent. They had passed their toughest test and were the first members of the Sikh brotherhood of the **Khalsa** (the pure ones).

Things to do

B *Sikh in traditional military uniform*

1 Study the information on the opposite page. Copy out these sentences and fill in the blanks.

a Gurus are ________ ________ who do not continue to be ________.

b As neither of his sons was fit to succeed him Nanak chose ________ ________ to whom he gave the name ________ meaning ________ ________.

c It was ________ ________ who founded the city of Amritsar.

d Guru Arjan prepared the Holy Book, the ________ ________ ________, for Sikhs to read. He also built the ________ ________ ________ at Amritsar.

e Guru ________ and Guru ________ were both put to death for their faith.

f Guru ________ ________ founded the Sikh brotherhood called the ________ which means the ________ ________.

2 Imagine that you had been one of the five men who volunteered to enter the tent with Guru Gobind Singh.

a Describe how you might have felt as you made up your mind and went towards the tent.

b Imagine that you had been a relative of one of these men. Describe your feelings as you heard the thud and saw the blood flowing out of the tent.

c Describe the excitement that you felt as the men came walking out of the tent with Singh.

d Why do you think that Singh carried out this test?

e What was he trying to find out about the men?

3 The Punjab area of North India is the home of the Sikh religion. Here some members of the faith still wear the traditional Sikh military uniform (see picture **B**).
Explain how the Sikhs believe that the warrior brotherhood began.

4 By tradition each Sikh is supposed to carry a small dagger or kirpan.

a What do you think the kirpan was used for when the Sikhs were a warrior brotherhood?

b What meaning do you think wearing a kirpan has for a Sikh today?

C *Cooking in the kitchen attached to the gurdwara*

Summary

Between Guru Nanak and Guru Gobind Singh Sikhs believe that there were eight other Gurus. A Guru is a man who is no longer reborn because he has managed to escape from the cycle of life and death.

7.1 *Religious festivals*

A *Hindu festival of dance*

These are many festivals in religion. These are occasions which allow people to give special significance to a religious event in the past. By trying to bring that event into the present people are able to understand its significance and meaning. In the festival of Passover, for example, Jews today relive events which took place some 4000 years ago.

More than anything else a festival is a time of remembrance and celebration. People set aside their normal pattern of life and work to come together. A festival is a special holiday time and as such usually has its serious and light-hearted sides (**A** and **C**).

At festival time people often exchange presents or send greetings cards. Special food and drink are prepared. Often people dress up in new clothes or fancy dress. Streamers, fireworks, firecrackers and bonfires are a common part of the celebrations. People often sing, play music, dance or take part in a procession. It is all part of the religious celebration which goes to make up a festival (**B** and **D**).

Most religions have more than one festival and these are held each year. Some of them are very serious because they are remembering sad events from the past. Others are happy occasions. Some, such as the Christian festival of Easter, combine both in the same festival.

So each festival has a meaning and its own special traditions to help people to remember what it means. The faith of the believers is strengthened as they listen to the stories they are told and take part in the traditions. As someone has said, 'It is a time when we remember the past, rejoice in the present and look forward to the future'.

B *Opening Christmas presents*

Things to do

C *A party at the Jewish festival of Purim*

1 Using the information on the opposite page answer these questions in your own words.
   - **a** How do festivals help people to understand more about the religious faith to which they belong?
   - **b** What do people often give each other at festival time?
   - **c** In what different ways do people take part in the celebrations?
   - **d** Which festival allows Jews today to relive events which took place 4000 years ago?
   - **e** Which Christian festival combines the serious and the light-hearted sides of a festival?

2
   - **a** Make a list of all the activities that people take part in at festivals as mentioned on the opposite page.
   - **b** Next to each activity on your list write down which is religious and which is not.
   - **c** Using three of the religious activities on your list explain why people celebrate in this way.

3 Pictures **B** and **D** show different sides of Christmas.
   - **a** Describe what you do on Christmas Day.
   - **b** Which of the things that you do on Christmas Day have a religious meaning?.
   - **c** Explain what the religious meaning is of as many of the Christmas Day activities as you can.

D *Carol singing*

Summary

By celebrating a religious festival people are trying to relive an important event from the past in their religion. A festival can be either serious or light-hearted but most festivals combine both aspects.

7.2 *The Passover*

Pesach or **Passover** is an important Jewish festival. It commemorates the delivery of the Jews from slavery in Egypt under the leadership of Moses some 4000 years ago.

Before the festival begins in the modern Jewish home every member of the family searches for any unleavened bread. This search is made into a game which the younger members of the family enjoy. If any is found it is destroyed. By doing this everyone is reminded that the Jews had to leave Egypt in such a hurry that there was no time for their dough to be leavened (to rise). So now Jews eat unleavened (unrisen) bread or **Matzah** during the eight days of the festival.

On the first two nights of Passover a special family meal called **Seder** is celebrated at home. The word Seder means *order* and refers to the special dishes on the table (see picture **A**). The family also reads the whole story of the journey out of Egypt from a book called the **Haggadah**.

As the story unfolds so the parsley is dipped in salt water. The salty taste is a reminder of the tears shed in suffering during slavery. Later the bitter herbs are dipped in charoset, a mixture of apples, raisins, almonds and cinnamon sprinkled with wine.

This paste suggests to everyone present the cement which the Jews used to build houses for their Egyptian masters. Its sweet taste is a reminder of the joy of the freedom which followed slavery.

During the meal everyone is told:

In every single generation it is a man's duty to regard himself as if he had gone forth out of Egypt.

In a very real sense this has actually happened. The land of Egypt represents slavery and the journey out freedom. Most men today live in that freedom. Those who do not, of whatever faith or none, are remembered towards the end of the service. In this festival all free men should rejoice in God:

Who performed for our fathers and for us all these wonders. He brought us forth from slavery into freedom . . . from darkness to great light. Let us sing before him, Hallelujah.

In Hebrew the word 'Hallelujah' means 'Praise the Lord'.

The roasted egg symbolizes new life whilst the shankbone of lamb stands for the lambs which were eaten in the last meal in Egypt.

A *The Passover meal*

Things to do

1 Copy the picture of the Seder plate into your book (**B**).

a What special foods are eaten at Passover?
b Why?

2 During the Seder service four questions are asked by the youngest child of the father. Here are the questions.

a 'Why is this night different from all other nights, for on all other nights we may eat leavened or unleavened bread but on this night only unleavened?'
b 'On all other nights we may eat other kinds of herbs but on this night only bitter herbs?'
c 'On all other nights we need not dip our herbs even once but this night we dip them twice?'
d 'On all other nights we eat either sitting or reclining but on this night we all recline?'

From the information given on the opposite page what answers would you give to questions **a**, **b** and **c**?

B *The Seder dish. There is a space for each of the six different foods*

3 This extract is taken from Exodus 6.6–7. During the Seder service four goblets are drunk to remind those present of the four ways in which God promised Moses that he would redeem (save) the people of Israel.

I will bring you out from under the burdens of the Egyptians, and I will deliver you from their bondage, and I will redeem you with an outstretched arm and with great judgements; and I will take you to Me for a people and be to you a God.

a What are the four ways in which God promised to save his people?

4 Read the story of the journey of the Jews out of slavery for yourself. It is found in Exodus chapters 12–14. Then imagine that you are a reporter on the journey out of Egypt. You have been sent to cover the whole event for your newspaper. Write up a record of the journey in three separate episodes giving a suitable headline to each of them.

5 Read the text on the opposite page and look at pictures **A** and **B** again. Describe in your own words what happens at Passover today. Here are some words to help you:

Seder dish   matzah   wine
Haggadah   questions

Summary

Passover is a great Jewish festival of freedom. It reminds Jewish people of the deliverance of their ancestors from slavery in Egypt. The Seder Meal, the central part of the festival, is celebrated at home. The meal is full of symbolic food to remind the worshipper of God's goodness to the nation of Israel.

7.3 Easter

A *Easter service*

Easter is the most important Christian festival of the year. It takes place in the spring and remembers the death of Jesus and celebrates his resurrection.

For forty days before Good Friday Christians prepare themselves for the festival during **Lent**. The emphasis in Lent is upon deep thought and self-denial reminding Christians of the forty days that Jesus spent in the wilderness being tempted by Satan.

The week before Easter itself is known as **Holy Week**. It begins with **Palm Sunday** when everyone in church receives a palm cross. This recalls the day on which Jesus rode into the city of Jerusalem on a donkey. On **Maundy Thursday** Jesus washed the feet of his disciples and ate his last meal with them. Many Christians celebrate Holy Communion on this day.

Then follows the most serious day of the Christian year called **Good Friday** when people remember the events leading up to the crucifixion of Jesus. It is called *Good* Friday because Christians believe that it was on this day that good completely triumphed over evil.

Two days later the mood completely changes. The darkness and horror of Good Friday gives way to the celebration and hope of **Easter Sunday**. The traditional greeting given by Christian to Christian on this day is

Christ is risen.

to which the reply is given

He is risen indeed.

B *Painting of 'Jesus Triumphant'*

On Easter Day churches are filled with flowers, light and spring colours (**A**). There is a feeling of joy and hope in the air.

C *Easter cards*

Things to do

D *Twentieth century reconstruction of Jesus carrying the cross, Mexico*

1 The phrases below are all jumbled up. Fit them together so they make a sensible paragraph. Then write it down in your book.

Two days later Easter Sunday is celebrated . . . in the forty days before Easter Christians keep Lent . . . On Good Friday they remember the death of Jesus on the Cross . . . the most important Christian festival is Easter.

2 Look at the cards in picture **C**.
- **a** What are the symbols associated with Easter that you can see on these cards?
- **b** Why do you think the first flowers of spring are associated with Easter?

3 Explain the following:
- **a** Lent
- **b** Palm Sunday
- **c** Good Friday
- **d** Easter Sunday

4 In this extract a young Christian was asked why Easter was the most important festival of the year for her. She answered:

I have always enjoyed Christmas time very much but as much for social as religious reasons. Now Easter – that is something altogether different. It has a feel to it that no other time of the year has. It is not as busy, noisy and hectic as Christmas. It is the time of the year when I try to sit down and reflect upon my religious faith more than at any other time. Somehow I seem to feel my faith more deeply at Easter than at any other time of the year.

- **a** What do you think are the main differences between the way that Christmas and Easter are celebrated?
- **b** Do you understand what this person means when she says that Easter has a different feel to it compared with any other time of the year?
- **c** What do you think there is about Easter which makes this young person more reflective about her Christian faith?

5 Look at picture **D**. Why do you think these Mexicans are acting out Jesus' life before the crucifixion?

Summary

Easter is the most important Christian festival. Good Friday recalls the day on which Jesus was crucified whilst on the first Easter Day he rose again from the dead.

7.4 *Eid ul Fitr*

A *Muslims breaking fast*

All events in the Muslim year are overshadowed by **Ramadan** and the feast which follows it. As the Qur'an commands them to do Muslims fast (go without food) between dawn and sunset for the whole month of Ramadan. By tradition the fast starts each day when it is possible to distinguish a white thread from a black one and ends when the two cannot be told apart (**A**).

The fast is taken very seriously indeed. During daylight hours no Muslim is allowed to take any form of food or drink. Also they must not smoke tobacco, have sexual intercourse or speak unkindly of anyone during Ramadan.

Certain groups of people are excused from taking part in the fast. They are young children, nursing mothers, old people and travellers. In the case of travellers they are expected to fast some other time.

In most religions a time of fasting is followed by a period of celebration. The end of the fast of Ramadan is anticipated eagerly by all those who have taken part in it. Before the celebrations can begin, however, every Muslim must give some charity to the poor. The amount laid down is the equivalent of two meals on behalf of every member of the household. The intention is to bring the joys of the Eid ul Fitr celebration to the poor and hungry as well.

Eid ul Fitr is the joyful and happy festival which ends Ramadan. It starts with special prayers, usually in the openair, so that as many people as possible can begin the festival together. After the prayers the worshippers greet one another, embrace and exchange best wishes (**B** and **D**).

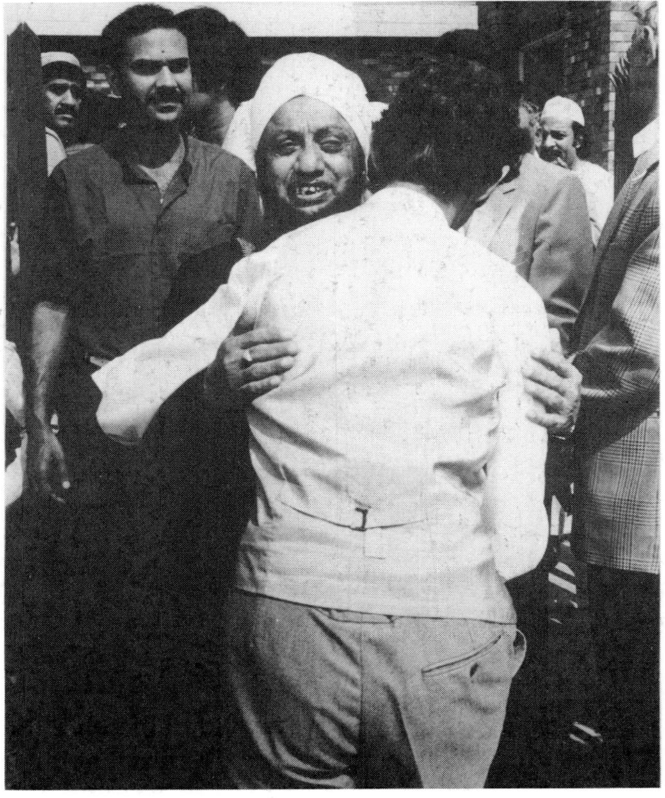

B *Hugging each other at Eid ul Fitr*

Following this friends and relations meet one another and presents are exchanged. New clothes are worn by everyone and there is often a party. Cards, like those in picture **C**, are sent to celebrate Eid ul Fitr.

It is the custom towards the end of the day, to visit the graves of dead relatives where a special prayer is said for all those who have died.

The word *Eid* means rejoicing and *Fitr* means charity. That sets the main theme for the festival.

C *Cards sent to celebrate Eid ul Fitr*

Things to do

D *Outside the mosque at Eid ul Fitr*

1 Each of these statements is either true or false. If true then copy it into your book as it stands. If false then copy in the correct version.

- **a** When a person fasts he goes without food or water.
- **b** During Ramadan Muslims fast from sunset to sunrise.
- **c** Each day's fasting traditionally begins when a white thread and a black thread can be told apart.
- **d** Travellers need not fast during Ramadan but are expected to fast at some other time.
- **e** Children, nursing mothers and the elderly are also excused from fasting during Ramadan.
- **f** Ramadan ends with the festival of Eid ul Fitr.
- **g** The word 'Eid' means charity and 'Fitr' means rejoicing.

2 This young Muslim is describing how he feels about the fast of Ramadan and the festival of Eid ul Fitr which follows it.

When we meet for Eid ul Fitr the purpose, above everything else, is to thank Allah (God). It is only by God's strength that we have been able to keep the 29 days of the fast. It is always a great experience for us all. Moreover it has not been a heavy duty for us to see the fast through. It has been an obligation which we have all willingly and joyfully accepted.

- **a** When the people meet for Eid ul Fitr what is their purpose above every other?
- **b** How have the people found enough strength to keep the fast?
- **c** How long does the fast of Ramadan last?
- **d** Does this young Muslim see the obligation to keep the fast as a heavy and unpleasant duty?

3 Young Muslims are introduced to the idea of fasting gradually by their parents. In the first year, for instance, they will probably only fast for one day.
Imagine that you are a young Muslim. What do you think are the main things that you would miss the first time that you fasted? Explain why?

4 Imagine that you are a young Muslim about to carry out the full fast of Ramadan for the first time. Write a letter to your grandmother in another country explaining your hopes and fears for the month that lies ahead.

Summary

Keeping the fast of Ramadan, which lasts a month, is a solemn responsibility for every Muslim. The fast is ended by the happy festival of Eid ul Fitr.

7.5 *Diwali*

The festival of **Diwali** is shared by Hindus and Sikhs. It takes its name from the main characteristic of the celebration. Diwali means 'cluster of lights' and light is to be found everywhere. Temples, places of work and houses are illuminated by clay oil lamps or candles (see pictures **A** and **B**). The symbol of light tells everyone that goodness has triumphed over darkness and evil.

For every Hindu family Diwali is a very busy time. The house must be made ready to welcome the god **Vishnu** (**C**) and his bride **Lakschmi**, who is the goddess of plenty. Houses are cleaned from top to bottom as husbands and wives renew their marriage vows to each other. Parents and children are reminded of their duties and responsibilities to each other.

The spirit of Diwali is also to be found elsewhere. Business is busy for a short time as people buy new clothes and household goods. Then the accounts for the past year are closed and new account books opened for the year ahead. There is music and dancing in the streets as floats pass by telling the traditional stories connected with the festival.

Although Sikhs celebrate Diwali in a similar way it is connected with important events in their own religious history. The foundation of the Golden Temple at Amritsar was laid by Guru Ram Das on this day in 1577. To celebrate the occasion the Temple is beautifully lit up by flickering lights so attracting thousands of visitors.

At this festival Sikhs are also celebrating the release of Guru Hargobind by the Mogul Emperor in 1620. Guru Hargobind was arrested because the Sikhs were seen as a threat by the Emperor. Many of the sixteen-year-old Guru's followers came to pray for his release outside prison. The fact that the Emperor let him go is seen by Sikhs as another example of the triumph of good over evil.

B *Flickering lights at Diwali*

A *Hindus celebrate Diwali*

Things to do

1 Copy and complete these sentences using the words below.

Vishnu dancing Amritsar Guru Hargobind cluster of lights Lakschmi marriage vows.

- a Diwali means ________ ________ ________.
- b At Diwali Hindu families prepare to welcome their god ________ and his bride ________.
- c ________ is an activity closely associated with the festival of Diwali.
- d At Diwali Sikhs remember the laying of the foundation of the Golden temple at ________.
- e At this time Sikhs also recall the release of ________ ________ from captivity.
- f At Diwali Hindu couples renew their ________ ________ to each other.

2 This is how one modern book describes the importance of dancing in the Hindu religion.

Hindu dancing is used to tell stories about the gods. Shiva is called the Lord of the Dance and it is claimed that the art originated amongst the gods before it was passed down to earth . . . Each movement has a meaning so as to tell the legend. Hand positions mean 'wind', 'holding a sword', 'a year' and so on. Brahmins (priests) must have white faces, female demons wear black robes and goddesses wear green with pearls. Dancers' faces indicate whether they are afraid, happy or angry.

- a For what purpose is Hindu dancing used?
- b Which Hindu god is called the Lord of the Dance?
- c From where do Hindus claim that dancing came from in the first place?
- d What kinds of things do the hand movements in the dancing mean?

3 Imagine that you are a young Sikh or Hindu who is about to celebrate Diwali in India. A pen friend in England has written to ask you about the festival and how you are going to celebrate it. Write a letter to him explaining the festival in some detail.

4 Compare Diwali with one of the other festivals you have learnt about in this book. In your own words write how the two festivals are similar and how they are different.

C *Nineteenth century painting of Vishnu, India*

Summary

Diwali is the only festival shared by both Hindus and Sikhs. It is the Festival of Light and symbolizes the triumph of light and goodness over the powers of darkness and evil.

7.6 *Ushering in the new year*

For Jewish people the New Year begins with the festival of **Rosh Hashanah**. This takes place in September or October. It is a holiday during which everyone looks back over the past year and forward to all that lies ahead. The **Shofar** (ram's horn) is blown in the synagogue to mark the beginning of ten days of deep thought and repentance (see picture **A**). According to Jewish tradition the shofar was blown at the creation of the world; when the Torah was given by God to Moses on Mount Sinai; the beginning of each new month and after all major battles.

A *Blowing the shofar*

During Rosh Hashanah special round **challahs**, or holiday bread, are baked. Their shape stands for the cycle of life starting at birth and ending in death.

At the holiday meal a piece of challah is also dipped in honey and everyone makes a wish for a sweet year ahead. The people also eat honey cake, honey biscuits and apple dipped in honey (see picture **B**).

B *Dipping apple in honey at Rosh Hashanah*

Rosh Hashanah is the first two days of repentance and the festival ends with the most serious day in the Jewish year, that is the **Day of Atonement** or **Yom Kippur**. On this day every Jew seeks the forgiveness of God and spends most of the time in the synagogue.

For Hindus their New Year festival, **Ungadi**, provides them with an opportunity to make a fresh start. The houses are cleaned carefully from top to bottom. Courtyards are swept and then decorated with flour patterns. During the morning bath the body is rubbed with sweet oils. New clothes are worn and those with money to spare give a new set of clothes to those who cannot afford to buy them

The festival of **Baisakhi** in April marks the beginning of the Sikh year (**C**). It celebrates the birth of the Khalsa brotherhood (see page 65). In the agricultural areas of North India it also marks the beginning of the time when the harvest is gathered in. The festival is so important, however, that the Sikh farmers only begin to collect in the waiting harvest upon which everyone depends when the celebrations of Baisakhi are over.

Things to do

C *Preparing the new flag at Baisakhi*

1 Pair up the tails (**i** – **v**) to the correct heads (**a** – **e**) in the following sentences.

- **a** The Jewish New Year festival is called . . .
- **b** The Jewish New Year festival ends with . . .
- **c** A morning bath is part of the festival of . . .
- **d** The Sikh year begins with the festival of . . .
- **e** The festival of Ungadi commemorates the beginning of . . .

- **i** Yom Kippur
- **ii** Baisakhi
- **iii** The Hindu year
- **iv** Rosh Hashanah
- **v** Ungadi

2 Look at picture **B**. Describe how you can tell that this is a picture at the time of Rosh Hashanah.

3 **a** Why do you think some people celebrate the New Year?
b Why do some people make New Year resolutions?
c Write down three resolutions people might make at the New Year.

4 Rosh Hashanah is a serious festival and during it a very solemn passage from the Torah is read out. It is the occasion on which Abraham was prepared to sacrifice his son Isaac (Genesis 22). See picture **B** on page 17.

At Rosh Hashanah all Jews remember their homeland of Israel. A woman who lost two sons in wars against Israel's enemies wrote to a friend:

Does this land, do the stones of the Wailing Wall, justify so many sacrifices – as Abraham was called upon to sacrifice his son Isaac? . . . Our joint answer is unequivocal – we had, and we will have, no other choice.

Explain in your own words what the woman meant by this comment.

5 Compare the ways in which the different religions on these two pages celebrate the New Year.

Summary

The blowing of a ram's horn marks the start of the Jewish New Year. The next ten days are spent in deep thought and repentance. To Hindus Ungadi represents a fresh start. The Sikh festival of Baisakhi comes at the beginning of harvest time.

Glossary

Abraham Considered by Jews to be the founder of their nation.
agnostic Someone who is not sure whether God exists.
Allah The Muslim name for God.
altar The central and most holy point in the east end of a church.
Angad Name given to Lehna after he was chosen by Guru Nanak to lead the Sikhs.
Anglican Someone who worships with the Church of England.
Ardas The common prayer in the Sikh service.
Ark The cupboard in the synagogue where the scrolls are kept.
atheist A person who believes that God does not exist.

BCE Before the common era.
Baisakhi Sikh festival celebrated in April.
Baptist Church A Non-Conformist Church which baptizes adults.
bimah A raised platform in the middle of the synagogue.
bishop Religious leader of cathedral and its surrounding Christian community.
Brahman The supreme Hindu spirit. Together with Vishnu and Shiva they form the Hindu Trinity.
Breaking of Bread The name for the Holy Communion service in a Non-Conformist Church.

CE Common era.
Cantor The professional singer who leads the worship in a synagogue.
cathedral Important church supervised by a bishop.
challah Special loaves of bread used during Jewish Rosh Hashanah festival.
chapel A Non-Conformist place of worship.
chauri Feather fan waved over the Granth in the gurdwara.
Chazan An official in a synagogue.
circumcision The removal of the foreskin of a boy's penis on the eighth day.
Church Centre A modern church built in a community centre.
Church of England The main Christian group in England.

Day of Atonement Most solemn day in the Jewish year.
Diwali Hindu and Sikh Festival of Lights.
Dewan Hall The prayer hall in a gurdwara.
Disciples Twelve men chosen by Jesus as his first followers.
dupattas Silk scarf worn as head covering by Sikh women in a gurdwara.

Easter Christian festival to remember the death and resurrection of Jesus.
Easter Sunday Day on which Christians celebrate the resurrection of Jesus from the dead.
Eid ul Fitr Muslim festival which comes at the end of the fast of Ramadan.
Exodus Journey of Jews out of slavery in Egypt 4000 years ago.

Ganesha The elephant-headed son of Parvati.
garbagriha Shrine room in Hindu temple.
Good Friday Christian festival which, as part of Easter, commemorates the death of Jesus.
Gospels First four books of the New Testament telling the story of Jesus.
Granthi Official who waves the chauri over the Granth in a gurdwara.
gurdwara A Sikh place of worship.
Guru A spiritual teacher in Hinduism and Sikhism.
Guru Granth Sahib The holy book of the Sikhs which stands in the centre of the gurdwara.
Guru Nanak Founder of the Sikh religion.

Haggadah A moral or devotional Jewish book.
Hegira Journey of Muhammed from Mecca to Medina in 662.
Holy communion The central act of Christian worship using bread and wine as symbols of the body and blood of Jesus.
Holy Week Events in the week leading up to Good Friday and Easter Sunday.

incense Sweet-smelling substance burned as part of religious worship.
Imam Man who leads prayers in a mosque.
Israel The homeland of the Jews.

Jesus Christ The founder of Christianity.

Judas Iscariot The disciple who betrayed Jesus.

Kaaba Black, cube-shaped shrine in Mecca, sacred to all Muslims.
Karah Parshad Food eaten at the end of a service in a gurdwara.
Kashrut Jewish dietary laws.
Khadijah Muhammed's first wife.
Khalsa Brotherhood of Sikhs.
kosher Food which is fit for a Jew to eat.
Krishna Favourite Hindu god.

Lakschmi Hindu bride of Vishnu. She is the primary deity of Diwali.
Langar Traditional meal which ends act of worship in a gurdwara.
Lehna The Sikh leader who succeeded Guru Nanak.
Lent The period of deep thought and repentance leading up to Easter.
Leviticus One of the early books in the Jewish Bible.
Lord's Supper Non-Conformist equivalent of Holy Communion.

mandir Hindu temple.
martyr Someone who dies for his or her religious beliefs.
matzah Unleavened bread eaten at the Jewish festival of Passover.
Maundy Thursday The day before Good Friday.
Mecca The holy city for all Muslims.
Messiah The spiritual leader that Jewish people are waiting for.
minaret Tower on a mosque from which the Call to Prayer is given.
minister The equivalent in a Non-Conformist church of a priest.
miracle An event for which there appears to be no natural explanation.
minyan The minimum number of ten men necessary for a Jewish service to be held.
Moses Prophet who led the Israelites out of Egypt.
mosque The meeting place for Muslims.
Muezzin Official who gives the Call to Prayer from the minaret.
Muhammed Prophet of Islam.

natalis The deathday of Christian saints.
Non-conformist English Churches differing from Church of England teachings.

Palestine Another name for Israel.
Palm Sunday Day which starts Holy Week and commemorates Jesus riding into Jerusalem on a donkey.
parable Story told to make a spiritual message clearer.
Passover Jewish festival held every year to celebrate the Exodus of the Jews.
Patriarch The highly revered 'father figures' of the Jewish religion.
Pesach Another name for the Passover.
Pharisees Main Jewish group opposed to Jesus.
prasad Sweetmeat given to Hindus by priest in worship.
prayer mat Mat used by Muslims when they are praying and not in a mosque.
prophet The name given to men who spoke to the people in God's name.
pulpit Raised platform from which a sermon is delivered.

Rakah Sequence of twelve positions adopted by a Muslim when praying in a mosque.
Ramadan Muslim month of fasting.
relic Bones of saint kept under altar in a church.
Resurrection Central Christian belief that Jesus rose from the dead.
Roman Catholic Church One of the main Christian groups.
Rosh Hashanah Jewish New Year festival.

Sabbath The Jewish holy day.
Seder Meal eaten by Jews on the first two days of Passover.
sermon Instruction delivered by vicar, minister, rabbi or imam.
Shiva The Hindu destroyer of the universe.
Shofar Horn blown at start of important Jewish festivals.
Siddur Jewish prayer book.
Sikh A follower of the religion established by Guru Nanak.
Simon Peter An important disciple of Jesus.
Sunday The Christian holy day.

Glossary

synagogue The Jewish place of worship.

takht Raised stand at one end of the gurdwara.
temple A Hindu place of worship.
Ten Commandments Most important part of the Law given by God to Moses on Mount Sinai.
Torah The Books of the Law which are the first five books of the Jewish Scriptures.
turban Traditional male Sikh head covering.

Ungadi Hindu New Year festival.

Vishnu The Hindu preserver of the universe.

Yom Kippur The Jewish Day of Atonement.

Books and addresses

Here are some useful books and addresses to help you find out more about each of the religions covered in this book.

Christianity
The Christian World
A. Brown (Macdonald)

The Christians' Book **
and *Exploring the Bible* **
From the Chichester Project: P. Curtis (Lutterworth)

Look at churches A. Duggan (Hamish Hamilton)

British and Foreign Bible Society,
146 Queen Victoria Street, London EC4V 4BX

Christian Education Movement,
2 Chester House, Pages Lane, London N10 1PR

Church Information Office, Church House, Deans Yard, London SW1P 3NZ

Hinduism
The Hindu World (Macdonald)
and *Hinduism* (Batsford)
P. Bahree

Hinduism
V.P. (Hemant) Kanitkar (Wayland)

A Handbook of Hinduism for Teachers **
D. Killingley (Grevatt & Grevatt)

Hindu Centre, 39 Grafton Terrace, London NW5

Indian Government Tourist Office, 21 New Bond Street, London W1 ODY

Judaism
The Jewish World
D. Charing (Macdonald)

Understanding your Jewish neighbour
Myer Domnitz (Lutterworth)

Thinking about Judaism
Myer Domnitz (Lutterworth)

Jews: Their Religious Beliefs and Practices **
A. Unterman (RKP)

Jewish Education Bureau, 8 Westcombe Avenue, Leeds LS8 2BS

Jewish National Fund, Youth and Education Department, Rex House, 4 – 12 Regent Street, London SW1Y 4PG

Jewish Information Service, 34 Upper Berkeley Street, London W1H 7DG

Islam
The Muslim World (Macdonald)
and *Islam* (Batsford)
R. Tames

Mosque: Its importance in the life of a Muslim
and *Muslim Festivals and Ceremonies*
Rashid Ahmad Chaudri (The London Mosque)

Minaret House, 9 Leslie Park Road, Croydon CR0 6TN

Muslim Educational Trust, 130 Stroud Green Road, London N4 3RZ

Sikhism
A Sikh family in Britain
W. Owen Cole (Pergamon)

The Way of the Sikh
W.H. McLeod (Hulton)

The Sikh World
Daljit Singh & A. Smith (Macdonald)

Sikh Cultural Society, 88 Mollison Way, Edgware, London HA8 5QW

Sikh Missionary Society, 10 Featherstone Road, Southall, Middlesex